A.E. HOUSMAN

Other *Border Lines* Titles

I.m. Tom & Babs Mason
(I didn't forget)

A.E. HOUSMAN

Keith Jebb

Border Lines Series Editor
John Powell Ward

SEREN BOOKS

SEREN BOOKS is the book imprint of
Poetry Wales Press Ltd
Andmar House, Tondu Road
Bridgend, Mid Glamorgan

British Library Cataloguing in Publication Data

Jebb, Keith
   A.E. Housman. – (Border lines, series)
   I. Title   II. Series
   821.912

ISBN 1–85411–049–7
ISBN 1–85411–050–0 (paperback)

The publisher acknowledges the financial support of the Welsh Arts Council

Typeset in Plantin by Megaron, Cardiff
Printed and bound by
The Cromwell Press Limited,
Broughton Gifford, Melksham,
Wiltshire

CONTENTS

List of Illustrations

Series Preface

The Border country is that region between England and Wales which is upland and lowland, both and neither. Centuries ago kings and barons fought over these Marches without their national allegiance ever being settled. In our own time, referring to his own childhood, that eminent borderman Raymond Williams once said: 'We talked of "The English" who were not us, and "The Welsh" who were not us.' It is beautiful, gentle, intriguing, and often surprising. It displays majestic landscapes, which show a lot, and hide some more. People now walk it, poke into its cathedrals and bookshops, walk on, fly over or hang-glide from its mountains, yet its mystery remains.

In cultural terms the region is as fertile as (in parts) its agriculture and soil. The continued success of the Three Choirs Festival and the growth of the border town of Hay as a centre of the secondhand book trade have both attracted international recognition. The present series of introductory books is offered in the light of such events. Writers as diverse as Mary Webb, Raymond Williams and Wilfred Owen are seen in the special light — perhaps that cloudy, golden twilight so characteristic of the region — of their origin in this area or association with it. There are titles too, though fewer, on musicians and painters. The Gloucestershire composers such as Samuel Sebastian Wesley, and painters like David Jones, bear an imprint of border woods, rivers, villages and hills.

How wide is the border? Two, five or fifteen miles each side of the boundary; it depends on your perspective, on the placing of the nearest towns, on the terrain itself, and on history. In the time of Offa and after, Hereford itself was a frontier town, and Welsh was spoken there even in the nineteenth century. True border folk traditionally did not recognize those from even a few miles away.

Today, with greater mobility, the crossing of boundaries is easier, whether for education, marriage, art or leisure. For myself, who spent some childhood years in Herefordshire and much of the past ten crossing between England and Wales once a week, I can only say that as you approach the border you feel it. Suddenly you are in that finally elusive terrain, looking from a bare height down on to a plain, or from the lower land up to a gap in the hills, and you want to explore it, maybe not to return.

This elusiveness pertains to the writers and artists too. Did the urbane Elizabeth Barrett Browning, just outside Ledbury till her late twenties, have a border upbringing? Are the 'English pastoral' composers, with names like Parry, Howells, and Vaughan Williams, English, or are they indeed Welsh? One wonders whether border country is now suddenly found on the English side of the Severn Bridge, and how far even John Milton's *Comus*, famous for its first production in Ludlow Castle, is in any sense such a work. Then there is the fascinating Uxbridge-born Peggy Eileen Whistler, transposed in the 1930s into Margiad Evans to write her visionary novels set near her adored Ross-on-Wye and which today still retain a magical charm. Further north: could Barbara Pym, born and raised in Oswestry, even remotely be called a border writer? Most people would say that the poet A.E. Housman was far more so, yet he hardly ever visited the county after which his chief book of poems, *A Shropshire Lad*, is named. Further north still: there is the village of Chirk on the boundary itself, where R.S. Thomas had his first curacy; there is Gladstone's Hawarden library, just outside Chester and actually into Clwyd in Wales itself; there is intriguingly the Wirral town of Birkenhead, where Wilfred Owen spent his adolescence and where his fellow war poet the Welsh Eisteddfod winner Hedd Wyn was awarded his Chair — posthumously.

On the Welsh side the names are different. The mystic Ann Griffiths; the metaphysical poet Henry Vaughan; the astonishing nineteenth century symbolist novelist Arthur Machen (in Linda Dowling's phrase, 'Pater's prose as registered by Wilde'); and the remarkable Thomas Olivers of Gregynog, author of the well-known hymn 'Lo he comes with clouds descending'. Those descending clouds . . . ; in border country the scene hangs over-head, and it is easy to indulge in inaccuracies. Most significant perhaps is the difference to the two peoples on either side. From England, the border meant the enticement of emptiness, a strange unpopulated land, going up and up into the hills. From Wales, the border meant the road to London, to the university, or to employment, whether by droving sheep, or later to the industries of Birmingham and Liverpool. It also meant the enemy, since borders and boundaries are necessarily political. Much is shared, yet different languages are spoken, in more than one sense.

With certain notable exceptions, the books in this series are short introductory studies of one person's work or some aspect of it. There are no footnotes or indexes. The bibliography lists main sources referred to in the text, and sometimes others, for anyone who would like to pursue the topic further. The authors reflect the diversity of their subjects. They are specialists or academics; critics or biographers; poets or musicians themselves; or ordinary people with however an established reputation of writing imaginatively and directly about what moves them. They are of various ages, both sexes, Welsh and English, border people themselves or from further afield.

The poetry of A.E. Housman is being, as they say, rediscovered. Not much had appeared on him for many years, but a number of factors have led to renewed interest. New material on his homosexuality, and new attitudes to homosexuality generally, go along with the publication of Christopher Ricks's publication of the collected poems and selected prose as recently as 1988, to make an account such as the present one not merely welcome but inevitable. As Keith Jebb's account makes clear, this is at least partly because the dual aspects of Housman's life and work — creative poet and dry-as-dust classical scholar, public Oxbridge professor and private lover of males — can now been seen in parallel far more than, for example, was possible in Richard Perceval Graves' albeit useful biography. This is Keith Jebb's first book, and in its combination of firm authority and relaxed approachability it is a remarkable debut. Keith Jebb is a poet, was born and raised (unlike Housman) in Shropshire itself, and is currently engaged in research at Oxford on modern poetry.

John Powell Ward

Author's Acknowledgements

I would like to thank Archie Burnett of Oxford Polytechnic, for giving me the benefit of his wide knowledge of Housman and the poems, particularly with regard to the text of the posthumous verse; his forthcoming definitive edition of the poems will end decades of confusion and error. Thanks are also due to Mark Jenner, who led me to the work of Jeffrey Weeks, which proved so important. Howard Cheese of Ludlow Museum helped me to locate photographic material for the book. All writers on Housman must owe a great debt to the work of Paul G. Naiditch in ascertaining the facts and fictions of Housman's life; I have acknowledged this where appropriate. I would also like to thank J.P. Ward, not only for entrusting me with the task of writing my first book, but for being a supportive and encouraging editor and consultant.

Any faults in the book are my own responsibility, as are all the opinions I express. I am aware of sometimes going against the grain of a consensus of critical opinion on Housman; this is not out of the wish to say something different, but because I believe this consensus avoids issues which need to be confronted, and which complicate the accepted view of what kind of writer and personality Housman was.

I would also like to thank Helen Kidd and the kids for putting up with the chaos of having another writer in the house.

Introduction

In many ways he was the Philip Larkin of his day: wrote little, published less and lived a "dull" academic sort of life, while at the same time being considered, by conservative literary opinion of the time, the best poet in England. Both men kept a low profile in literary circles, avoided reading or discussing their own work; but whereas Larkin had his followers in Hull, Housman kept his acolytes at a safe distance, usually America. Both were popular poets, and both died bachelors, with reputations for pessimism founded on their verse, but which friends saw offset against a surprising sense of humour and a love of at least some of the things of life. The comparison is, of course, deceptive: though many of their attitudes — to death, to religion – could be compared, you could no more imagine Housman fumbling with a pair of cycleclips "in awkward reverence" than you could imagine Larkin putting himself in the place of the criminal about to be hanged; but each performed a similar function as a poet in his time: they wrote, often about death, in a language poetry audiences understood; they forged no new language for poetry and made no great claims for their art, being naturally conservative; they each left — some would put this differently — a handful of important poems.

Since his death in 1936, the character and personality of A.E. Housman have caused as much, if not more, comment than his poetry. He is seen as a man divided: divided between the pedantic academicism of the classical scholar and the sentimental fatalism of the romantic poet; and divided between the aloof bachelor who shunned personal attachments and the lonely, repressed homosexual, living on the memory of his one, unrequited love. Besides numerous biographical sketches (many by people who knew him personally) and a handful of full-length biographies, critical comment on the poems themselves has been dominated by speculation about their origins and roots in Housman's emotional make-up, and about their possible relevance to known and unknown events in his life. It may be inevitable that this will happen to any writer who attempts to lead a very private life, and who leaves behind little in the way of information and comment about himself; but it is no less unfortunate for that. His poetry has tended to become a kind of cryptic diary, as important for its gaps and omissions as for anything it actually does say. The shadow of that one love, Moses Jackson, is cast across the whole of his work, poetic and scholarly, while wider issues, such as what it might have meant to be a homosexual writing love poetry at the turn of the century, have been largely ignored.

Even within the field of biography itself, a largely unbalanced approach has produced some notable distortions. Literary people, which biographers generally are and Housman certainly was not, find it difficult to view the minute research and intricate mechanics of textual criticism as anything but purgatory, and then tend to project their own feelings on to Housman and paint what he saw as his real life's-work as a form of exile from the poet's life he could have led, or as a disappointed corner he retreated to when love was lost. The idea that Housman may have actually enjoyed his work might be pretty indigestible, but the industry and pride with which he approached it mean that anyone who wants to deny it had better have a pretty good case, and the fact that you find the thought of such work — which of course you know little about — dull and dry is not one. Even worse is the allied assumption that because his love for Jackson remained unanswered, and because there is no good evidence that anyone else ever took his place, that therefore Housman led an unhappy and perhaps even tragic life. This is a facile and rather reductive logic; there is some evidence for unhappiness, some for happiness with his lot: but that he came to terms with his emotional situation seems to me to be the most reasonable, if least interesting, conclusion.

These are some of the pitfalls that I hope to avoid in writing this book. It is a general introduction to Housman, his life and his work, centring on his poetry, but trying to do justice to all the other subjects which impinge upon it. He was, essentially, a Victorian minor poet, but one of the best of his kind; neither he nor his poetry pretended to any form of greatness; like Larkin he belonged to a tradition that sees poetry as an amateur pursuit. His career (if you can call it that) serves as an example of how multi-faceted one historical period can be. When *Last Poems* was published it was well reviewed and immediately popular, a book for its times, full of poems which (though in the main written earlier) could be read in the context of the recent Great War. That was 1922, and it is now usual to see the time reflected in that other book of the year, T.S. Eliot's *The Waste Land*. There should be no surprise in this; Housman was no anachronism, nor was Eliot ahead of his time, but each responded to quite different needs and conditions that were just as contemporary as each other. I have just called Housman a Victorian poet; but like millions of Victorians he outlived his Queen and stayed the same person, belonged to the same world he didn't see change that much. By his own account the Great War changed very little for him and he would not have been unique: he represents the conservative strain in literary history which is always a very real present force, as it is now.

I
The Man

Biography

Alfred Edward Housman was born on 26 March 1859 in the Valley House, Fockbury in Worcestershire. He was the first child of Edward Housman and his first wife Sarah (née Williams). His father, a qualified solicitor, was second son of Thomas Housman, a clergyman, but effectively the eldest since a family scandal involving an adolescent Thomas (Edward's older brother) and the family nanny. Sarah Jane Williams was the daughter of the Rev John Williams, Rector of nearby Woodchester, and Elizabeth (née Cooke). Rev. Williams had been to Oxford and was something of a poet and classical scholar; his daughter was a lover of literature who combined High Anglican piety with the talent for writing occasional witty verses ridiculing people she knew.

Edward and Sarah were married in June 1858, a few months after her father's death, and moved briefly into the Valley House, owned by Edward's father. But quite soon after the birth of Alfred they moved on to Bromsgrove, a couple of miles away, and Perry Hall, vacated by the death of Captain John Adams, Government Agent for Stamps, one of Edward's distant relatives and his former employer. It was in this large well-appointed house in the shadow of Bromsgrove church that Alfred's family grew rapidly around him. Robert was born in 1860, Clemence in 1861, followed by Katharine (1862), Basil (1864), Laurence (1865) and finally George, who became known by his second name, Herbert (1868).

These brothers and sisters seem to have formed a happy and mutually supportive group, with Alfred very much the leader. There is an example told by his brother Laurence, of Alfred demonstrating the motions of the planets:

> One day he took two of us out on to the lawn, and there placed us as astronomical characters. I was the sun, my brother Basil the

17

> earth, Alfred was the moon. My part in the game was to stay where
> I was and rotate on my own axis; Basil's was to go round me in a
> wide circle rotating as he went; Alfred, performing the move-
> ments of the moon, skipped round him without rotation. And that
> is how I learned, and have ever since remembered, the primary
> relations of the sun, the earth, and the moon (*A.E.H.* p.22)

This early real interest in astronomy probably took some part in Alfred's decision to edit the Roman astronomer-poet Manilius, many years later: he certainly became a consummate astronomical and astrological scholar.

Meanwhile Edward continued a rather part-time approach to his work as a solicitor. He was a man of many pastimes but no firm commitment, a fact that became ruinous as time went on. But for the time being the couple were happy and the family grew into the expectations of respectable upper middle-class society, and the routines of church and daily family prayers (servants included) in the dining room. Alfred won a scholarship as a day-boy at Bromsgrove School and was clearly very intelligent. Sarah, however, was not physically strong and the strains of frequent childbirth weakened her. Her health broke down and after a protracted illness she died, of cancer, in 1871. Alfred had acted as both nurse and confidant to his mother during her final months, and her death effectively ended his childhood. He later said of his relationship with his mother at this time that "she used to talk to me as if I were a grown up person, and told me many things of her early life" (*A.E.H.* p.24). When it was clear that she had not long to live, Alfred was sent away, to spend his twelfth birthday with old family friends, the Wises of Woodchester where, on that birthday, he received a letter from his father telling him of his mother's death.

The event had a profound effect on Housman. He later said that he became a deist at twelve and an atheist at twenty-one. The letter from his father had relayed to him his mother's wish that he should not lose his faith. Apparently the family had already observed the beginnings of a process of loss of faith in response to Sarah's decline. But because, perhaps as much as any other reason, they were there when he needed them, and because they were close friends of his mother's, he formed a lifelong bond with the Wises of Woodchester which made that village the home he would continue to visit until his final years. The family's German governess, Sophie Becker, became an especially close friend, one of two or three close emotional attachments which Alfred made in his whole life. They remained in contact, even after she returned to Germany before the War, until she died, in her nineties, in 1933.

In 1873 Edward married his cousin Lucy Housman; nearing fifty and seven years his senior, she had never been married, but now took on a large family of children she did not know. She had been Sarah Williams's best friend and had introduced Edward to her. By all accounts Alfred took up the role of mediator between Lucy and the younger elements of the family, a supportive effort which became the base of a firm friendship and mutual respect. His earliest surviving letter is a long description of impressions of London, from a visit he made in 1877. They had a long and continuous correspondence, Alfred always addressing her 'My dear Mamma.'

The year before his marriage, Edward had moved his family to Fockbury House in Fockbury, also still known to some at the time as The Clock House, though the clock referred to had gone. It was a seventeenth century house in the country. The tenant had died and Edward, one of the trustees to the property, was now depriving himself and his brothers and sisters, the other joint owners, of this source of income. It was the first of a series of ill-considered and at times barely legal decisions which eventually ruined his family's finances and his own standing as a 'man of honour'. But it was a pleasant seventeenth-century house, lacking many of the facilities of Perry Hall, but with plenty of space for the children, and for the time being Edward could play the country squire.

At Bromsgrove School the replacement of the headmaster Dr Blore gave Alfred his first real mentor, Herbert Millington, described by Laurence as "For clever boys with a taste for the classics, excellent. For boys with less interest and of lower ability, quite the reverse" (*A.E.H.* p.36). (Laurence did not get on well with him.) This was another acquaintanceship that was lifelong.

Alfred began to lead his brothers and sisters in literary games, poems, stories and plays, and he began to compose both humorous and serious verse. Some of the plays were performed, mainly unrehearsed, before a fairly underwhelmed family audience. Hardly surprising, since they seem to have been composed by Alfred doling out parts for the others to write, keeping the best character for himself and occasionally helping one or two of the others along. One of the first poems Laurence remembered having "written" was actually one of Alfred's cast-off compositions, which he half-succeeded in convincing his younger brother was really his own. At school Alfred won prizes for Latin and English composition, finishing the sixth form as head boy.

His two school prize-winning poems, 'The Death of Socrates' and 'Paul on Mars Hill' are long narrative poems, showing no real signs of the kind of poet Housman was to become, which some of his private juvenilia does. Housman himself came to regard an earlier poem which did not win, about Sir Walter Raleigh, as a better piece of writing. Perhaps this was because the poem is a little more vigorous and less rhetorical. As with most poets' school efforts they are exercises in competence with metre and rhyme, and with the building of a poetic argument: little more could be expected of them. A comparison of passages may show something of the difference between Alfred the competition-poet and the same boy making verses for his own satisfaction.

> Though weeping followers on the earth stand dumb
> With sorrow, unto them no dawn has come,
> On them no lifted veil has shed the light;
> With lisping thought and visionary sight
> They wait in twilight. But the day shall be
> When a frail bark shall bear across the sea
> One, in the wisdom of whose solemn eyes
> A deeper, clearer well of light shall rise,
> And on the hill thy feet so oft have trod,
> He shall in fulness preach thine UNKNOWN GOD.
> (*A.E.H.* p.31)

These are the concluding lines to 'The Death of Socrates', written when he was fifteen and his first published poem, appearing in *The Bromsgrove, Droitwich and Redditch Weekly Messenger* for 8 August 1874 ('Paul on Mars Hill' was mentioned for winning the prize the following year, but not printed). The following lines come from a poem written when he was perhaps sixteen:

> Summer: and after summer, what?
> Ah, happy trees, that know it not.

> Would that with us it might be so!
> And yet the broad-flung beech-tree heaves
> Through all its slanting layers of leaves
> With something of a sigh. Ah, no!
> 'Tis but the wind that with its breath
> To them so softly murmureth:
> For them hath still new sweets in store,
> And sings new music evermore.
> Only to us its tones seem sighs,
> Only to us it prophesies
> Of coming Autumn, coming death.
> (*A.E.H.* pp.33–34)

These lines, for all their crude emotion, have some interesting touches — the description of the beech-tree leaves, for instance. Also they produce an unusual denial of the pathetic fallacy, that crediting of inanimate things with human emotions that was a staple of much romantic poetry. In declaring unequivocally that such notions are our projections, he foreshadows one of his last published poems, *LP* XL, 'Tell me not here, it needs not saying', his farewell to nature:

> For nature, heartless, witless nature,
>   Will neither care nor know
> What stranger's feet may find the meadow
>   And trespass there and go,
> Nor ask amid the dews of morning
>   If they are mine or no.

Here the denial forms the twist in the tail of a poem which first sets up the picture of nature as female enchantress. The poems are so similar in tone and theme that they give added strength to the common assertion about Housman that his poetry shows little development over the years.

One of the prizes he won at school was a book which he later said had first turned his mind to classical studies "and implanted in me a genuine liking for Greek and Latin" (*P.&P.* p.297). It was Millington's gift of a copy of *Sabrinae Corolla*, a book of translations of English poetry into Latin and Greek, edited by B. H. Kennedy, Headmaster of Shrewsbury School and renowned classical scholar. It is a significant coincidence that in 1911 Housman became Kennedy Professor of Latin at Cambridge.

In 1877 Edward Housman was forced finally to sell Fockbury House and move his family back into Perry Hall, which he had already taken mortgages out on in deals which were unauthorized by his brothers and sisters and counter to his father's will. In a rather dubious episode in which Ted Wise basically baled him out, he had effectively made Perry Hall his own property. Eventually these dealings caused a rift between Edward Housman and Ted Wise which forced Alfred into a kind of estrangement from Woodchester for about eight years between 1878 and 1886, naturally a cause of some sadness to him.

Meanwhile Alfred won a scholarship to St John's College, Oxford. It was decided he should try for Oxford rather than Cambridge, apparently because his English was not considered strong enough, a decision which meant his academic career would not start where attitudes towards classical studies would always be closer to his own than Oxford's rather more literary approach. He matriculated in 1877, sending Lucy a long amusing letter about the ceremony at Oxford and his first impressions of it:

> As to keeping the statutes contained in the violet cover, you may judge what a farce that is when I tell you that you are forbidden to wear any coat save a black one, or to use firearms, or to trundle a hoop, among other things. (*Letters* p.12)

This sense of the ridiculousness of it all became more contemptuous as he became acquainted with the standard of Oxford scholarship. He is reported to have attended just one lecture by Benjamin Jowett, Regius Professor of Greek, before coming away "disgusted" by his disregard for the niceties of scholarship (*Gow* p.5).

His earliest Oxford friend was his fellow classics scholar Arthur Pollard. He later became acquainted with the man who, he told Laurence years afterwards, "had more influence on my life than anyone else" (*De Amicitia* p.39). M.J. Jackson was a sciences undergraduate and athlete. Like Housman and Pollard he had a college scholarship. He struck a somewhat philistine attitude towards the arts, and his sporting exploits could not have been more of a contrast with Housman, a rather slight figure who had been called 'Mouse' at school by boys who pretended to tread on him accidentally. This was clearly some attraction of opposites. During his first year at Oxford, he made a number of contributions of humorous prose and verse to an undergraduate magazine *Ye Rounde Table*, under the pseudonym 'Tristram'. This amounts to the bulk of his Oxford literary endeavours; he made two appearances in the magazine *Waifs and Strays* in 1881 with 'Parta Quies' (*MP* XLVIII) and 'New Year's Eve' (*AP* XXI), but apart from these the only serious poem he is known to have written during his Oxford days is 'Iona', his failed Newdigate Prize attempt of 1879. The prize, for English verse, has a set subject: Housman worked through the night and produced something not unlike his Bromsgrove prizewinning poems. Next morning in chapel the lesson included the words "we have toiled all the night, and have taken nothing". It is said he came third.

Initially his work went well: the first part of the course contained the subjects (Greek and Latin translations) most suited to him and in the Moderations examinations of 1879 he came out with a First. What happened next is the subject of much conjecture, un-supported assertion and general bewilderment. We know the ultimate result for sure: in the final, Greats examinations of 1881 Housman achieved the distinction of an outright fail; he was, in the parlance, 'ploughed'. The whole list of possible reasons for this turnabout, along with the evidence for and against them, is admirably set out in Paul G. Naiditch's *A.E. Housman at University College: The Election of 1892* (E.J. Brill, Leiden, 1988), at once the best and most unreadable book about Housman. Most speculation surrounds the role of Moses Jackson: did Housman realise the homosexual nature of his feelings for him just before the examinations? Were his feelings rejected? Did they spend too much time together when Housman should have been working? But there are many other factors to be considered.

During their fourth year Pollard, Jackson and Housman took a set of rooms in St Giles, opposite St John's College. Jackson's First in science was already secure, and he had little need of continuous study. Pollard used to work in his room during the evenings, but remembered that the other two would spend long hours talking in the sitting room. What evidence there is suggests that Housman's work started to become less than exemplary; one anecdote runs that after College collections (unofficial examinations) in 1880–81, the

Senior Tutor "made a harmless remark of Housman the occasion for informing us all that he was *not* a genius!" (Pollard in *Brom.* p.32). This may suggest that the problem was of longer standing than some shock or revelation just before Greats. On the other hand, it was only six days before his Finals that he learned his father had suffered a stroke. This would be cause enough for worry, even if he did not already know of Edward's financial problems, of his increasing alcoholism and his growing eccentricity. But we know that he eventually came to lose all respect for his father, and it is possible that news of the illness came as an added worry, but not something he was utterly unprepared for.

To add to this there are factors to do with Housman's course of work at Oxford, and with the requirements of the exam. He had already begun a study of the manuscripts of the Roman poet Propertius, work which was totally irrelevant to Greats. Subjects which were relevant, like Greek philosophy and political economy, were of no interest to him, and he seems to have all but refused to study them. His attitude to Oxford scholarship in general at this time could be summed up as arrogant. Perhaps he had decided that textual criticism was his area of study and that he would follow it at all costs. This way he may have committed academic suicide, but he may have been too overconfident to realise it.

But even this may barely explain the extent of his failure. On some papers he hardly attempted to answer questions. Any notion that the examiners had been too hard on him seems to be dealt with by Housman himself, who said years later that they "had no option" but to plough him (*Gow* p.6). In the end we are left with an insoluble mystery. In a way there are too many good reasons why Housman might have done badly. The most dramatic possibility — that he suddenly realised the homosexual nature of his feelings for Moses Jackson, and that the subsequent emotional crisis destroyed his chances of success — while it cannot be discounted, and while it might explain how he failed so spectacularly, is the one for which any evidence is purely conjectural. Pollard was Housman's friend and lived in the same house, but apparently saw no signs of such a crisis in the young man's personality. He put the disaster down to lack of work and over-confidence.

However, Housman returned home a changed person:

It was probably the blow of his failure which caused him to withdraw completely into himself, and become a silent and impenetrable recluse in the midst of his own family during the eighteen months which elapsed before he left home to take up his Civil Service appointment in London. (*A.E.H.* p.56)

His family could hardly recognize him. "If sympathy was what he feared to receive on his return from Oxford, he took the best means to deprive himself of it" (*A.E.H.* p.57) Laurence wrote. During this period he studied successfully for his pass degree as well as passing the Civil Service examination. Millington helped him out by giving him some teaching at Bromsgrove school, so he could make some contribution to the shrinking family coffers. The dining room was the one room in the house the family could afford to heat, and Alfred studied there, with the distractions of the household all around him. He turned down one Civil Service post in Dublin, before accepting the second, as Higher Division Clerk in the Patent Office in London. Moses Jackson was in the same Office, working as Examiner of Electrical Specifications. Obviously it was a happy coincidence, if it had not been partly engineered by the two friends. Soon after moving to London late in 1882, he was moving in with Moses and his brother Adalbert at their lodgings in Bayswater.

The legend of Housman's stay at the Patent Office is one of a young man doing time-serving clerical work during the day and spending his evenings in the British Museum writing a series of brilliant articles for the classical journals. The first of these articles appeared in 1882, on 'Horatiana', and another in 1883; but then there is a four year gap before the next. The fact is that most of the articles upon which Housman's early reputation was based were published between 1889 and his meteoric rise to a professorship at University College, London in 1892. Other things were happening in his life.

Little is known about his time at the Office; he appears to have done his work efficiently — despite his own claims that he did "as little as possible" there — and to have got on well with his colleagues. One of these, John Maycock, paid him a remarkable tribute in a letter of congratulation on his appointment at University College:

As a rule English people never allow themselves to say or write what they think about anyone, no matter how much of a pal he may be. Well, I am going to let myself loose. I like you better than any man I ever knew. There is, as far as I could ever discover, absolutely no flaw in your character as a man, and no one would ever hope for a better friend. I don't say this only on my own account, but I have seen how you can stick to a friend like you have to Jackson. I mean not stick to him in the sentimental sense of not forgetting him although he is right out of your reach. (*A.E.H.* p.92)

Maycock here refers to something which I doubt he even knew the half of, and which we can only piece together a few fragments of, this "sticking to Jackson".

In the autumn of 1885 something happened in the Jackson household which caused Housman mysteriously to disappear for a week. Moses went as far as to write a worried letter to Edward Housman. When he reappeared he was soon to move out, and after a stay at Northumberland Place he moved to 17 North Road, Highgate, 'Byron Cottage', (where he was to write *A Shropshire Lad*), and the landlady Mrs Hunter he was to remain loyal to until he left London. It may be significant that the period during which Housman's production of published articles dried up completely corresponds roughly with that between his moving in with the Jacksons and Moses Jackson's departure for India, to become Principal of Sind College, Karachi in 1887. I say it may be significant, but there is also the possibility that in these years he laid down the groundwork for the flood of material that was to come. But I will go into this period in more detail in the next chapter, as it is important to any understanding of Housman and his work.

Jackson visited England infrequently during the following years. During one extended stay in late 1889 he married, keeping the event secret from Housman until after the ceremony, in fact until after he had left the country again. But the two friends continued to correspond until Jackson's death in British Colombia in 1923. Among Housman's papers after his death were found two letters, kept together and obviously treasured. One was Jackson's last letter to him, written from his deathbed, the pencil carefully traced over by Housman in ink. The other was Maycock's letter of congratulation.

In 1892 Alfred Goodwin, who had held the combined chairs of Latin and Greek at University College, London, died. The College decided to advertise the two chairs separately and Housman applied principally for the Latin post, stating that he would like to be considered for the Greek if unsuccessful in his first choice. With his letter of application went seventeen testimonials, ranging from eminent scholars like Henry Nettleship, Professor of Latin at Oxford, J.E.B. Mayor, Professor of Latin at Cambridge, and the German Wecklein, through to his friend Arthur Pollard and his old headmaster Herbert Millington, testifying to his English style and his teaching experience respectively. But the vast majority of these references were from scholars of the highest calibre, many of whom only knew of him through his published writings. Such was the impact that his work in the classical journals had made, that he could boldly declare, without any attempt at explanation: "in 1881 I failed to obtain honours in the Final School of Litterae Humaniores. . . ". He got the job.

In the 1890s professorships at non-Oxbridge universities were not the positions they are now. The classics department at University College had two teachers, the professors of Greek and Latin (Housman and William Wyse, until the latter was replaced a couple of years later by Arthur Platt) who were expected to do all of the teaching and lecturing, as well as taking part in the day-to-day running of the College and trying to keep up with their research interests. It was a number of years before Platt and Housman were granted the services of an assistant. Housman became heavily involved in the activities of the College in a way that his later reputation for aloofness would be hard pressed to account for. He was a frequent attender of various committee meetings, in fact probably the most frequent of any of the members of the academic staff, serving on a number of sub- and occasional committees. He was Dean of the Faculty of Arts and Law from 1895–6 to 1896–7, and from 1899 he was a member of the College Council. As a member of the Senate he served on a large number of committees engaged in various aspects of the administration of the College.

But he also gave good service to another aspect of College life, described in his introduction to a posthumous collection of essays by his friend and colleague Arthur Platt:

University College London, like many other colleges, is the abode
of a Minotaur. This monster does not devour youths and maidens:
it consists of them, and it preys for choice on the Professors within
its reach. It is called a Literary Society, and in hopes of deserving
the name it exacts a periodical tribute from those whom it
supposes to be literate . . . . Platt, whose temper made him
accessible, whose pen ran easily, and whose mind was richly
stored, paid more of this blackmail than most of his colleagues,
and grudged it less . . . . (*P.&P.* p.344)

Housman, whose temper made him less accessible, whose pen did
not run easily, and who probably grudged it with a good deal of wry
resignation, paid more than his fair share of this tribute. He read
papers on Matthew Arnold, the Spasmodic School, Erasmus
Darwin, Robert Burns, Tennyson and possibly Swinburne. These
were destroyed in accordance with the terms of his will by
Laurence, but part of the Arnold and a typescript of the Swinburne
(which may not have been delivered to the Literary Society) have
survived. They show him in a fairly exuberant mood. They have
the same incisive wit and devastating sarcasm as appear in the most
notorious passages from the prefaces to his classical editions; but
because they were written for delivery in a social situation, and
because he was indulging in a pursuit he did not feel himself
entirely suited to making judgements in, the tone is more light-
hearted and there is no malice even where the wit is sharpest. They
also show that, despite his frequent disclaimers, he was a more than
adequate literary critic. Here is an example from the essay on
Swinburne:

The fact is that, whatever may be the comparative merits of the
two deities, Liberty is by no means so interesting as Aphrodite,
and by no means so good a subject for poetry. There is a lack of
detail about Liberty, and she has indeed no positive quality at all.
Liberty consists in the absence of obstructions; it is merely a
preliminary to activities whose character it does not determine;
and to write poems about Liberty is very much as if one should
write an Ode to Elbow-room or a panegyric on space of three
dimensions. And in truth poets never do write poems about
Liberty, they only pretend to do so: they substitute images.
(*P.&P.* pp.279–80)

This may be wobbly political theory, but it makes good fun and sense with a real literary problem. Housman's attitude to such writings is summed up by his comment to a friend who, having heard the Swinburne lecture, asked if it might be published:

> and, on hearing that it was to be destroyed after his death, ventured to suggest that if Housman thought it bad he would already have destroyed it himself. "I do not think it bad," said Housman; "I think it not good enough for me." (*Gow* p.22)

An audience was one thing, posterity another. The arrogance of the reply is an instance both of Housman's intellectual vanity (which he acknowledged) and, I would suggest, of his dry sense of humour. One year Housman presented the Foundation Oration of the College Union Society, delivering a paper on Thomas Campbell. This Oration was customarily printed:

> We noticed as Housman went on, that he continued tearing up little bits of paper: we noticed because such nervous fidgetiness was unlike him. When the President, at the end, made the usual request for the manuscript, Housman replied that it had been destroyed. As the address proceeded he had been tearing up each page of his discourse after the other. (*Chambers* p.373).

But before this career could get under way, the newly-appointed Professor of Latin (he began work in the autumn of 1892) had to make his first appearance before his College. As the most recently arrived member of the academic staff he had to lecture before the joint Faculties of Arts, Law and Science. He lectured on the reasons for acquiring knowledge, steering a course between the contrasting assumptions of the arts, with their notion of 'humane letters', and the Sciences and their idea of the utilitarian ends of knowledge. He called the one side arrogant, and dealt with the other by fairly scathing treatment of the philosopher Herbert Spencer. He concluded the Introductory Lecture with the argument that the pursuit of knowledge is its own end and that "knowledge in itself is good for man". (*P.&P.* p.273). Standing before the united faculties he included an apt and unifying rallying cry:

> There is no rivalry between the studies of Arts and Laws and Science but the rivalry of fellow soldiers in striving which can

> most victoriously achieve the common end of all, to set back the
> frontier of darkness. (*P.&P*. p.274)

Many thought the lecture a brilliant debut, though there was some
disapproval and even affront at his brusque treatment of Herbert
Spencer, whose reputation was then very high. Housman himself
later criticised it as "rhetorical and not wholly sincere". He had,
after all, ventured confident assertions in an area where such
confidence is difficult honestly to hold. Although it was not
published until 1933 it was privately printed by the College in
1892, perhaps the only Introductory Lecture to be granted this
honour. In a preface to the reprint he wrote:

> the Council of University College, not I, had the lecture printed. I
> consented, because it seemed churlish to refuse. (*P.&P*. p.505)

Housman's teaching at University College seems to have been
more than adequate, but he was not an inspiring tutor. Remarks
from former students paint the picture of a reticent and fairly dry
character, somewhat aloof, setting his students high standards.
There are stories of him sending female students away in tears,
such were his demands and the forthrightness with which he
expressed them. He was also prone to forgetting his students'
names, something he joked about in his farewell speech to the
College, excusing himself that if he had remembered the names, he
might have forgotten something more important, such as elements
of the subject he was supposed to be teaching, like the difference
between the second and fourth declensions.

Given the heavy teaching burden, his published output during
these years was very high. A series of major papers on Propertius in
1893 put the seal on a project begun while he was still an
undergraduate and continued through his time at the Patent Office.
Besides numerous other articles, mainly on Latin sources (though
he still continued some work on Greek), this period saw the
publication of his edition of Juvenal (1905) and of the first book of
the *Astronomica* of Manilius (1903), a poem which was to occupy
him for thirty years. It was Manilius that he determined would be
the monument to his scholarship, and it is still considered to be one
of the major works by an English Latinist.

Housman's personal life while he was at the college remains rather shadowy. However, we have the testimony of friends and colleagues which tend to suggest a more approachable and convivial character than he later became at Cambridge. But there is one big proviso: nobody seems to have got really close to him, certainly among the academic staff and students. Most of the stories about his social life revolve around the Literary Society with its comradely crossing of swords between colleagues before an interested body of students, and around his exploits as an after-dinner speaker. Platt and W.P. Ker, the Scots English Professor, were his main friends amongst the academic staff. Housman paid generous tribute to Platt in his preface to Platt's posthumous *Nine Essays*, as well as quoting a "credible witness" for the following amusing anecdote about his exploits at the Zoological Gardens:

> I remember going to the giraffe-house and seeing a crowd of children watching a man who had removed his hat while the giraffe, its neck stretched to the fullest capacity, was rubbing its head backwards and forwards upon the bald crown. When the object of this somewhat embarrassing affection turned his head, Platt's features were revealed. (*P.&P.* p.346)

A student at the College during this period, R.W. Chambers, leaves a vivid account of this triumvirate. It includes a Literary Society meeting where Housman, speaking about Burns, included a few jibes at Scotsmen, for the benefit of the Glaswegian Ker. The audience expected the usual fireworks from a man whose humour was every bit as dry as Housman's. Instead he simply replied, "Forgiveness is the last refuge of malignity. I will not forgive Professor Housman" (*Chambers* p.372). This won the day. Chambers pays both men a high compliment:

> In these debates Housman, like his colleague Ker, had the power which belongs to the great, as it belonged to Dr. Johnson: if his pistol missed fire he knocked you down with the butt end. (*Chambers* p.370)

Clearly, as Graves has pointed out, at this period Housman was enjoying belonging to a community, but outside of college life he kept himself very much to himself, so that few people got to see his private sanctum at 'Byron Cottage.'

During the early 1890s a handful of events occurred which must have had a great effect on his life. On 12 November 1892 Adalbert Jackson died of typhoid fever, aged twenty-seven. His death is commemorated in the posthumously published poem 'A.J.J.' (*MP* XLII). They had maintained a close friendship since Moses left for India. On 27 November 1894 Edward Housman died at the age of sixty-three. By this time, as Laurence put it, "the poor man managed to outlive the respect and appreciation of everybody but himself". He had taken to drink; fallen prey to various get-rich-quick schemes of his own devising and left his estate in ruins. But there is no reason to suspect that the event did not weigh heavily upon his eldest son, despite or perhaps because of these circumstances. He had his stepmother to think of as well, the person who had unselfishly held the family together in the most difficult of situations.

Then in 1895 came the Wilde trials. Oscar Wilde's ill-advised attempt at a libel action against the Marquis of Queensberry backfired, ending in disaster for Wilde and an outbreak of fear amongst the homosexual population of England. But the trials also served to focus a group of people who had so far attained very little sense of community and common purpose, and Wilde himself quickly became a figurehead for those who shared what he called, speaking in his own defence, "the love that dare not speak its name".

These events and the departure of Moses Jackson in 1887 (the date of Queen Victoria's Jubilee and the title of the first poem in *A Shropshire Lad,*) span the writing of the poems in A. E. Housman's first volume of verse, none of which appears to have been written before 1890. The book appeared in February–March of 1896 in an edition of five hundred copies published by Kegan Paul at Housman's own expense. It had previously been turned down by at least one publisher, Macmillan, possibly on the advice of their reader John Morley. Alfred's old friend Arthur Pollard suggested Kegan Paul, his own publisher, who had a policy of producing small books of verse at the author's expense. It was Pollard who also suggested the title, the original being 'Poems by Terence Hearsay.' The implications of this change may go farther than just giving the book a better and more memorable title; they have a lot to do with the notion of the poet Terence Hearsay as a figure in and behind the poems — but I will discuss this later.

Although it gained a handful of good reviews, the book was not an instant success, three hundred and eighty-one copies selling in the first year. But the appearance of A.E. Housman the poet came as something of a surprise to everyone who knew him, even to members of his family who thought his production of serious verse had dried up a dozen years before. Laurence relates his particular surprise when, having just begun to publish verse of his own, he suddenly discovered his brother to be the better poet, the same brother who had already been corresponding with him, offering judicious criticisms of his own poems. His sister Kate's reaction was of a different kind, more related to the change that had come over Alfred since his failure in Greats: "Alfred has a heart!"

Writing formed the basis of a particular relationship between Alfred and Laurence, based on badinage, some mutual respect and an acceptance, apparently mutual, of the superiority of the elder brother's literary productions. There was also the fun of being mistaken for one another, usually in the form of the prolific Laurence being mistaken for the more anonymous, homonymous author of *A Shropshire Lad*. Two years after the publication of this first edition, Laurence found that six copies remained unsold and

> I bought the lot, gave some away, and then thirty years later, after telling Alfred that I was going to have a ramp with the second-hand book-market, I contrived to sell one 'unopened' copy for £12, the next for £20, the next for £30, and the last, which he obligingly inscribed for me to make it unique for £70. It sold later in America for £80, which I believe constitutes the top price up to date. Proud of my exploit, I wrote to Alfred offering him the proceeds as more rightfully belonging to him than to me.

Housman's reply ran as follows:

> At our last Feast I had the new Dean of Westminster next to me, and he said he had long been wanting to thank me for the amusement he had derived from my writings, especially about Queen Victoria and her ministers. So if I bring you money, you bring me fame. (*A.E.H.* p.81)

In 1898 a second edition of *A Shropshire Lad* appeared, published by a keen young publisher called Grant Richards, nephew of Herbert Richards, one of the examiners who had ploughed Housman in Greats. He was a fan of Housman's work, and it was he who approached the poet, asking for permission to take over the rights to the volume. Housman obliged, waiving his entitlement to any royalties on the book. Richards remained Housman's publisher, in one way or another, via bankruptcy, for the rest of his life. They developed a convivial acquaintanceship, based in the main part on a mutual love of good food and wine: Housman became a notable connoisseur and frequenter of the best restaurants in Europe. Richards's book *A.E. Housman 1897–1936* is an exhaustive and occasionally amusing account of this peculiar friendship between an amiable rogue and a solitary, often unapproachable academic (who never seemed unapproachable to Richards), peppered with letters from Housman chiding the publisher on the mistakes of printers and his occasional playing fast-and-loose with the poet's copyright, all written with the dry humour of one for whom exasperation has become second nature. Take the following, August 17, 1906 (Moring's had just purchased the rights to *The Smaller Classics* series):

> Alexander Moring Ld. have written to me asking to be allowed to continue to include *A Shropshire Lad* in *The Smaller Classics*. I have refused and have told them how atrociously you behaved in ever including the book in the series, and how glad I am to have the chance of stopping the scandal.
>
> I suppose you won't be in Paris between Tuesday and Saturday. I shall be at the Normandy. (*Richards* pp.72–73)

Nothing was taken personally between them.

Although Housman's reputation as a poet steadily increased over the years, he steadfastly refused to play the man of letters. All the same he became acquainted with some of the leading writers of his day, including Thomas Hardy, Robert Bridges, Edmund Gosse and Wilfred Scawen Blunt. But it always remained difficult for people to reconcile the academic with the poet, and in this sense perhaps Laurence was a useful presence on the scene, since another Housman, even without the frequent confusions, could not help but diffuse some of the attention away from himself.

The turn of the century brought a few years of bad news for the family. In 1901 Herbert, the youngest brother, died fighting in the Boer War, and in 1905 a short illness killed his brother Robert, aged forty-four, who caught a chill while standing in a stream to take a photograph. Finally, Lucy Housman died in 1907 at the age of eighty-four. On the other hand, Alfred had discovered a fresh outlet for his energies in overseas travel, taking his first trip, to Paris, Rome and Naples, in 1897. He still lived with his old landlady Mrs Hunter, though she moved to Pinner in 1905, making Housman's daily journey to the college in Gower Street considerably longer. But this congenial way of life, combining a decent London social life with a private, almost reclusive domestic arrangement, was soon to come to an end.

In December 1910, J.E.B. Mayor, Professor of Latin at Cambridge University died, having continued working to the age of eighty-five. Housman was one of the few prime candidates for the job, although his acerbic reviews and prefaces had won him a certain notoriety, not to mention a few enemies. Fortunately, perhaps, testimonials were not required this time. In spring 1911 he was elected to the post and to a fellowship at Trinity College. A few months after the election the post became officially known as the Kennedy Professorship, after Benjamin Hall Kennedy in whose honour it was established in 1869 but who had refused to allow his name to be used. Housman was entering a lineage he respected: Kennedy was the editor of the book *Sabrinae Corolla* which had so influenced the youthful Alfred; the Chair's first encumbent, H.A.J. Munro had been pestered by an under-graduate A.E.H. asking for his photograph and had given him generous, though negative, replies; Mayor had been one of the academics who supplied testimonials for Housman's application for the University College London chair nineteen years earlier. An undergraduate failure had finally reached the summit of his profession.

His Cambridge Inaugural Lecture (first published in 1969 under a title — 'The Confines of Criticism' — supplied not by Housman but by John Carter) was delivered in the Senate House on 9 May 1911. In it he pays what is, for somebody as hard to please as he was, virtual homage to his three predecessors. He then goes on to delineate the limits of textual criticism as a science, and emphatically not a branch of literature; but not an exact science either, since its results, unlike true scientific data, cannot be submitted to experimental proof. I will discuss the contents of the essay later, in the chapter on Housman's scholarship and prose; safe to say now that it was well received in Cambridge. It was not published in his lifetime because he could not verify a reference he made to the manuscript of Shelley's poem 'Lament' (1821), about which he has since been proved right.

He had left London with a mixture of regret and relief. His teaching burden would now be much lighter, reduced to a course of lectures every term. But living in College would force him into a rather unwonted proximity with other people; not that these would all be strangers: he had been a member of the Cambridge Philological Society since 1889 and had regularly attended their meetings. Perhaps to keep up some illusion of seclusion he moved into rooms up forty-four steps in Whewell's Court, a gloomy neo-Gothic building on the opposite side of Trinity Street from the main college buildings, which everybody except Housman, who liked that style of architecture, seemed to find depressing. It wasn't quite a hermitage, but it helped. When he left University College some of his former pupils presented him with a silver loving-cup inscribed with two of his own lines (from *ASL* LXII):

> . . . malt does more than Milton can
> To justify God's ways to man.

One of his farewell comments before the College, at the Professors' Dining Club, was on a similarly bibulous theme: "Cambridge has seen many strange sights. It has seen Wordsworth drunk; it has seen Porson sober. Now I am a greater scholar than Wordsworth, and a greater poet than Porson, so I fall betwixt and between." (quoted in *Graves* p.97).

Although a good public speaker, Housman always claimed to have no small-talk, and the evidence is pretty solid that he was right. On the other hand he was apparently quite a good listener, if somebody was prepared just to be listened to, and in this way he could cope with people whom others found difficult. But most people found Housman difficult — at least until they knew what to expect and not to be offended by his silences. Numerous people testify to the near impossibility of getting anything out of him at Cambridge high table dinners. This was variously interpreted as unfriendliness, rudeness, chronic shyness, or just a plain lack of anything to say. It is not easy for us to choose between these alternatives, nor to say very clearly where one ends and another begins (since shy people, for instance, can be very rude as a means of self-protection), but one little episode may throw some light on how it was for him. The following correspondence took place after the first and possibly only (though they were both pall-bearers at Hardy's funeral) time the two men ever met, at dinner one evening:

> Dear Professor Houseman,
> I am sorry about last night, when I sat next to you and did not say a word. You must have thought I was a very rude man; I am really a very shy man.
> Sincerely yours
> J.M. BARRIE.

Housman replied swiftly:

> Dear Sir James Barrie,
> I am sorry about last night, when I sat next to you and did not say a word. You must have thought I was a very rude man; I am really a very shy man.
> Sincerely yours
> A.E. HOUSMAN.
> P.S. — And now you've made it worse for you have spelt my name wrong

(anecdote quoted in *Richards* p.385)

Perhaps this shows the degree of self-consciousness behind Housman's persona.

However, he could at times be decidedly waspish. Evan Pughe, an old Trinity man billeted in Whewell's Court during the First World War, tried to tell Housman how much he had enjoyed his poetry and received a stern rebuff: "The kindest action the Dons have ever done me has been never to mention my poems" (Richards p.324); this from a man who, conversely, was very glad of the wide audience his poems had gained, was careful to assure they were available cheaply, and was particularly pleased with his readership amongst members of the army.

While so much attention is paid to his loneliness, the supposed tragedy of his life and the fact that most people found him extremely difficult to know, what is often overlooked is that fact that some people knew a totally different Housman — certainly the Wises of Woodchester, and his brother Basil and wife Jeannie, both non-intellectual and easygoing types whom Alfred visited frequently after the First World War. Similarly Grant Richards and his family saw the more open side of his nature. In 1916, in fact, he went on holiday with them to Cornwall:

> Certainly, if it were true that Housman did not take kindly to the society of women, did not like children, and had no affection for animals, he would have shown signs of discomfort. It was a fact that he seemed to enjoy all the incidents of what was in many ways a children's holiday, only showing signs of impatience when he found himself involved in some infantile larking or boisterous horse-play. (*Richards* p.151)

Clearly the professor was easier with people he knew he could relax with and trust: most, if not all, of those who thought of him as unfriendly either met him very rarely or only did so at relatively formal occasions, like college dinners, when he was often not on good form — although he did gain some reputation for telling dirty jokes.

Misogyny is another charge laid against Housman that it is difficult to defend him against. He spoke of "the deplorable sex" and once wrote:

> Man regards woman with intellectual contempt and sexual passion, both equally merited. Woman welcomes the passion but resents the contempt. She wishes to be rid of the discredit attached to her little brain, while retaining the credit attached to her large bosom. (quoted *Graves* p.87)

This is a surprisingly blunt piece of chauvinism from a man who had taught women at University College and had apparently made no complaints about doing so. His Cambridge friend Withers relates the following anecdote:

> "Where would you expect her to be?" he was once asked at table when savagely inveighing against a hostess who, after presiding at

a dinner-party of men, joined them later in the drawing-room.
"In the pantry!" he snapped. (*Richards* p.395)

Perhaps the prejudices of a conservative-minded, Victorian-
reared bachelor, but they do appear to have caused a lot of comment
at the time, suggesting he was a more belligerent chauvinist
than most. He was always courteous with women he did not know
well, but gallantry, that heterosexual trait, would be beyond
him. Counterbalancing this is the evidence of his respect for,
and emotional attachment to, a small number of individual women.
His mother, obviously, was the first of these. Helping to nurse
her during her last months made this bond stronger, while
his enforced absence at the actual time of her death must have
been hard to take. When he died Laurence found that he
had hoarded every scrap of paper with her writing on it. Lucy
Housman, escaping the negative role so often associated with the
step-parent, was another woman for whom he showed considerable
respect, loyalty and genuine friendship. She and not his father
was the recipient of most of his undergraduate letters home. He
was, as I have said, enormously helpful in making her feel a part of
the family when she first arrived, and always seems to have
appreciated the sacrifices she made for the children, and of course
for Edward. With Sophie Becker there seems to have been more of
a meeting of minds: she was intelligent, well read and independent
minded (although some mixture of all three could be said to
characterise both his mother and Lucy) and, with the Wises, was a
stabilising presence when he needed it most, after his mother's
death.

In his social encounters with women, Housman was frequently
charming. Sometimes he even found it easier to talk socially with
women than with men. Joan Thomson, daughter of Sir J. J.
Thomson the Nobel Prize-winning physicist, seemed to have an
insight into his introversion:

> If genuine affection and sympathy were offered him, however,
> Housman responded in full and gave unexpected proofs of deep
> feeling. He would give of his very best in conversation with
> someone who cared for him, even if that were a comparatively
> uneducated person. His intellect that would expose ignorance in

the very clever could make someone of most ordinary capacity appear gifted under the influence of his stimulating talk. (in *Richards* p.447)

Perhaps his defenders overcompensate for him. But Joan Thomson certainly seems to have had an understanding with Housman which suggests she might be right, and that what he needed most from people was the unembarrassed expression of genuine affection. Another of the discoveries made after his death was in his copy of T.E. Lawrence's *Seven Pillars of Wisdom*. In the margin by the following passage he wrote, "This is me":

> I was very conscious of the bundled powers and activities within me; it was their character which hid. There was my craving to be liked — so strong and nervous that never could I open myself friendly to another. The terror of failure in an effort so important made me shrink from trying; besides, there was the standard; for intimacy seemed shameful unless the other could make the perfect reply, in the same language, after the same method, for the same reasons.

In other words, he was striving for the impossible and, ever the good self-analyst, he knew it, but could do little about it. Is it no coincidence that both were homosexuals living in repressive circumstances? Although it obviously paints a picture of a man struggling with an emotional problem, I hope this evidence breaks up the more usual image of A.E.H the split-personality — the repressed homosexual who retreated from unrequited love into the pedantic world of scholarship and whose human feelings could only find vent in his poetry; the figure painted in Auden's poem: "Deliberately he chose the dry-as-dust, kept tears like dirty postcards in a drawer" (*Collected Shorter Poems 1927–1957*). The main thing this leaves out of the picture is his introvert's constant self-analysis, of which I believe there is a good deal of evidence. It also discounts the relationships he did manage to experience; and the whole issue of his sense of humour. What I am saying is that most interpretations of Housman's character are basically simplistic.

This is a suitable moment to mention Housman's tastes in pornographic literature. He read widely in this area: Cleland's

Fanny Hill. Lawrence's *Lady Chatterley's Lover,* much of Frank Harris's work, etc.; and he amassed a large collection of material on sado-masochism and in particular flagellation. This ranges from Swinburne's *Whippingham Papers* to a lot of rare and obscure continental works. Some of them are basically homoerotic, such as Baron Corvo's letters, much of it at least partly so.

In 1930 he wrote to Grant Richards:

> I return the D.H. Lawrence, with thanks for your perilous enterprise on my behalf. It did not inflame my passions to any great extent, but it is much more wholesome than Frank Harris or James Joyce. (*Richards,* p. 251)

The Lawrence book is, of course, *Lady Chatterley's Lover,* and the Joyce is *Ulysses,* both of them banned at the time. It would be interesting to know just what Housman meant by "wholesome" here. Housman wrote in 1922 that he had "scrambled and waded" through *Ulysses* "and found one or two half-pages amusing" (*Richards* p.197). Perhaps he found its intellectuality self-indulgent, even a bit morbid, against which the Lawrence is much more straightforward, though also more straightforwardly misogynist. Clearly he read it with the same eye as the British authorities, as potential pornography, rather than a work of literature: it seems that he read many works because they were banned. This shows the flexibility of the notion of pornography: it can, depending on prevailing social mores, be used to cover a very wide range of material. Perhaps pornography is not so much a type of literature or art (in the widest sense) as a way of reading.

A degree of sado-masochism seems to have been an element in much of the homoerotic literature of the time, and obviously this had something to do with the repression of homosexuality and the need to expiate a very real sense of guilt which many homosexuals experienced. Such fantasies could therefore be seen as a sexualization of the very real pain of being a homosexual, a moral and psychical pain. Housman's apparent interest in heterosexual pornography could be explained either as a latent bisexuality and/or an outlet for his misogyny, since almost all European and American pornography could be shown to be in some way misogynist. What I do not want to suggest is that Housman's homosexuality was inherently misogynist, a kind of rejection of women, or revenge against the mother, any more than hetero-sexuality is a rejection of and revenge against the father; although Freud's controversial theory of the Oedipus complex could be interpreted in just this way. It would be all too easy to say that Housman became a homosexual in order to 'punish' the mother he loved so much for dying so early. We can't know that this is even partly the truth, let alone the whole truth. What we can say is that a misogynist element in his character probably worked its way out on the level of sexual fantasy. The presence of this repressed element in his character could account for the apparent contradictions in Housman's attitudes towards women. But this is only speculation, hints towards understanding the man.

Incidentally, one of his scholarly articles, 'Praefanda', was a study of the use of indecent words by classical Roman poets. The essay was dropped at the last minute by *Classical Quarterly*, for obvious reasons, finally seeing the light of day in a German journal in 1931. It is, as befits Housman, a serious academic investigation.

His travels abroad became a regular feature of University vacations. After the first in 1897, he waited until 1900 for his second trip, which included a visit to Venice. He had a kind of love-affair with this city which lasted till about 1908. The fact that he always employed the same young man, Andrea (who had had one eye kicked out by a horse and had a large extended family to support) and frequently referred to him in letters as "my gondolier", has led some — in particular the biographer Richard Perceval Graves — to talk quite confidently about another love affair, of which there is no real evidence. He had other friends in Venice, the Englishmen Walter Ashburner and Horatio Brown. In 1904 he made his one trip outside of Europe, to Constantinople on the Orient Express. Meanwhile Housman's reputation as a gourmet spread to France, where the manager of the famous Paris restaurant Tour d'Argent, Frederic, did him the honour of naming a fish dish, *Barbue Housman*, after him.

The outbreak of the First World War did not stop him travelling. In March 1915 he travelled to the Riviera with Grant Richards: "Hitherto I have always refused to go to the Riviera, but now is my chance, when the worst classes who infest it are away", he wrote typically, having announced to the same friend: "On the 16th I shall be beyond the Channel or beneath it: more probably the former, for steamers seem to ram submarines better than submarines torpedo steamers" (*Letters* p.138). When he did cease to travel, abandoning a trip to France in April 1916 it was, he wrote to Richards, "not on account of mines and torpedoes, which I despise as much as ever" (*Letters* p.145), but because the Folkestone route was closed and he thought the Southampton–Le Havre route too long for the short holiday he had planned. After the War he chose another way of risking his life, becoming one of the early commercial airline passengers, flying to Paris in 1920. This became his regular way of getting to the Continent from then on, and only once did he deliberately refuse this mode of transport, in August 1929, the year before the fifth book of his Manilius was published:

> I am deserting the air on this occasion because my life, until my Manilius is finished, is too precious to be exposed to a 1/186,000 risk of destruction; even though they have already killed their proper quota for this year. (*Richards* p.250)

In 1919 he became a member of the exclusive Cambridge dining club, The Family, a group strictly limited to twelve people, who would each entertain the others in turn. He hardly ever missed one of their meetings, taking the trouble, when receiving them at Trinity, to prepare the salad himself.

In 1929 he refused the Order of Merit, explaining in his letter to the King's Secretary, with a quote from Admiral Cornwallis's reaction to a similar situation: "I am, unhappily, of a turn of mind that would make my receiving that honour the most unpleasant thing imaginable" (*A.E.H.* p.113). Later he was heard to joke, boastfully, "You know, it is really a great distinction to have refused the O.M." (Joan Thomson in Richards p.446). It was: he shared it with George Bernard Shaw. But the paragraph following the one I previously quoted from T.E. Lawrence's *Seven Pillars of Wisdom*, and by all accounts included by the "This is me" marginal note, supplies a more serious explanation:

> There was the craving to be famous; and a horror of being known to like being known. Contempt for my passion for distinction made me refuse every offered honour. I cherished my

independence almost as did a Bedoin, but my impotence of vision showed me my shape best in painted pictures, and the oblique overheard remarks of others best taught me my created impression. The eagerness to overhear myself was my assault upon my own inviolate citadel.

The two important paragraphs from Lawrence's autobiography suggest a complex web of self-reflexive strategies. At the risk of repeating myself, the idea that this all comes from his being "Heart-injured in North London" (to quote Auden's poem again) just does not fit. It seems to me to belong to an older strata of character formation, somewhere, say, between the early death of his mother and what Laurence Housman describes as "The Heavy Change" when he came back home from Oxford. What relationship this had to his sexual orientation, in an age when homosexuality and secretiveness were two sides of the same coin, is something we cannot say for sure, whatever the temptations to try. It is possible — but only possible — that the nature of his internal emotional defences would have made the actual expression of his homosexuality in a loving relationship virtually impossible. This would certainly give the lie to those who want to blame Moses's reaction to Alfred's feelings for his life's "tragedy".

Despite telling people for years that he now wrote little poetry, in 1922 another volume, pessimistically called *Last Poems*, finally appeared. It is true that his output had been generally low, one or two poems per year average at the most, although he had produced a flurry of poems about the time of the Boer War. In 1920 he tantalized Grant Richards with the possibility of a new volume, but this came to nothing at the time. Then the news of Moses Jackson's illness produced an effect in the poet similar to what he called the "continuous excitement" of 1895 when he wrote so many of the poems in *A Shropshire Lad*. His reputation had reached a high point during and after the Great War, partly due to the martial theme running through *A Shropshire Lad* which originally led Kegan Paul to suggest he turn it into a "romance of enlistment". He refused that; but during the war he joked that he wanted a copy of the book to save a soldier's life by turning aside a bullet: "Hitherto it is only the Bible that has performed this trick" (*Richards* p.155). While *A Shropshire Lad* did not join the Bible in this respect, Housman did keep a letter he received from an

American who had looked after a wounded British soldier during the war and had taken him a copy of the book only to find the soldier reaching for his own copy, tattered and bloodstained, and with three other Housman poems written in it.

Despite this, the war poetry in *Last Poems* belongs in the main to the Boer War, only 'Epitaph on an Army of Mercenaries' being an actual First World War poem. In an important late letter, answering a questionnaire from Maurice Pollet in 1933, he said: "The Great War cannot have made much change in the opinions of any man of imagination" (*P.&P.* p.469). It was the Boer War that made changes for Housman; his youngest brother Herbert, a sergeant in the King's Royal Rifle Corps, was killed in action in February 1900, and this led to a run of poems about death and soldiers, including 'Illic Jacet' (*LP* IV), 'Grenadier' (*LP* V) and the real poem for Herbert, 'Astronomy' (*LP* XVII):

> For pay and medals, name and rank,
>   Things that he has not found,
> He hove the Cross to heaven and sank
>   The pole-star underground.

as the second stanza runs, yoking his grief with his knowledge and love of astronomy, pitting the personal against the universal.

Last Poems appeared on October 19, 1922 in an edition of four thousand — a number decided by Grant Richards after discouraging noises from booksellers — but was such an instant success that by the end of the year a total of twenty-one thousand had been printed. Despite this instant popularity, it was generally recognized that this was more of the same stuff as his first volume, despite the quarter of a century that had passed. In fact, some of the poems had been written, or at least started, before 1896, and a few had originally been intended for the earlier book, including *LP* III, 'Her strong enchantments failing,' and *LP* XI, 'Yonder see the morning blink.' Housman was being hailed as perhaps the greatest poet in the country: it was the year of T.S. Eliot's *The Waste Land*.

The title of the volume gave notice that A.E. Housman intended to publish no more poetry during his lifetime. He was sixty-three. He had finally answered the years of pestering from people like Grant Richards, eager for a follow-up to *A Shropshire Lad*. He saw no prospect of more and perhaps the title was there to discourage anyone from pestering him again. But the next ten years saw him working as hard as ever. In August 1921 he delivered his lecture *The Application of Thought to Textual Criticism* before the Classical Association in Cambridge. In 1926 he brought out an edition of the works of Lucan, and in 1930 the fifth and final book of his edition of the *Astronomica* of Manilius.

Moses Jackson had died early in 1923 from stomach cancer. He had moved from India to British Columbia in Canada in 1911, to take up farming. When he died, Alfred had only recently sent him a copy of the newly-published *Last Poems*, including the poem 'Epithalamium', written in honour of Moses' wedding and some twenty-five years in the making. In the letter sent with it he wrote: "you are largely responsible for my writing poetry and you ought to take the consequences" (quoted in *Graves* p.189). Despite the years and this unusual friendship with a famous poet, Jackson had gained no more love of poetry than in his undergraduate days, and Housman knew it. But the dedication in the first volume of the Manilius is a twenty-eight line poem in Latin elegiacs to the man who had been, through much of Housman's life, a kind of guiding absence.

In 1933, rather against his better judgement, he accepted the task of delivering the annual Leslie Stephen Lecture. His own claims about the rarity of true literary critics would have made him wary of taking on that function himself; and despite a life spent in textual criticism, producing prefaces, reviews and articles all in English, he found English prose composition an extremely arduous task, and had only recently turned down Laurence's request for an essay on Coventry Patmore on account of the effort and stress it would involve him in. He also felt that his own powers were on the decline, and he was starting to suffer the first signs of ill-health. Completing his Manilius had really been the seal on his life's work — perhaps he took on this new task in order to give himself one more target to go for. What certainly must have motivated him was the opportunity to make some kind of definitive statement of his views on poetry. He had always kept himself on a tight rein in this respect, but this lecture, plus his letter in reply to a series of questions by Maurice Pollet, represent a kind of old-age loosening of the tongue, or perhaps a desire to set things straight. He had, throughout his life, a strong feeling for the notion of posterity, which shows itself in poems like 'To an Athlete Dying Young' (*ASL* XIX) and the Woolwich Cadet poem (*ASL* XLIV). The monument to his classical scholarship had already been erected.

He told Percy Withers that while writing the lecture "his days had been unabated torment. He had awakened every morning to the dread of a task to which he could bring no heart, and a struggle that had never given him a moment's satisfaction, or could so give" (Withers p.102). Afterwards he made it clear that he regretted doing it, feeling that it was this effort which had helped put an end to his good health. But on 9 May 1933 he stepped up to lecture in the Cambridge Senate House for the second and final time, and he clearly enjoyed himself. *The Name and Nature of Poetry*, as he entitled it, had the effect of a counter-blast to the new generation of Cambridge literary critics, represented by I.A. Richards and F.R. Leavis, even though it never mentioned them, nor even alluded to their existence. The story goes that afterwards, as everybody filed out of the hall, Richards was heard to mutter, "This has set us back ten years." He was wrong: although it was an instant success, gaining positive notices from, of all people, T.S. Eliot, in a few years it was of interest only to students of Housman's work. But for the older generation of Cambridge academics its essentially Romantic and anti-intellectual view of poetry served as a rallying cry.

During the last three years of his life he continued to work, keeping up with his termly courses of lectures, despite increasing ill-health. In the autumn of 1933 he spent a few days in the Evelyn Nursing Home in Cambridge, the first of a number of such stays. His heart had shown signs of weakness; but 1934 was in some ways a better year. In June 1935, however, he was back in the Evelyn. He recognized the symptoms of Cheyne-Stokes breathing from Arnold Bennett's novel *Clayhanger*, a condition which made breathing very difficult, particularly at night. "The kind and foolish comrade that breathes all night for me," was failing. He wrote to Percy Withers, himself a physician:

> "You probably know all about Cheyne-Stokes breathing . . . : sleepless nights spent in recurrent paroxysms of failure of breath, which can be combated if one is broad awake, but which overwhelm one if one dozes." (*Letters* p.372)

Withers collected him from the Evelyn and took him to stay with himself and his wife for a few days. At dinner on the first evening he was animated, lively and amusing before the Withers's guests; but for the rest of the visit he spent his nights in extreme discomfort and his days reading quietly in the sitting room. He wrote to Mrs Withers afterwards: "I was glad to hear that you said I seemed happy while with you, for indeed the fact was so, and everything conspired to give me peace and enjoyment" (*Letters* p.373). After leaving them he went to join members of his family for a trip to his childhood home, the Clock House, where Laurence was opening a fete. Later in the summer he even managed a final vacation in France. His time was marred by a bad blow on the head he gave himself entering a taxi. The wound had to be stitched, but he continued his holiday, wearing a cap over the dressing. He still managed to enjoy himself.

But back in England he was complaining, always without self-pity, about the effort involved in staying alive, and that he did not wish it to continue any longer. Earlier, in June, he had even half-jested in a letter to Laurence that he still went up his forty-four stairs two at a time in the hope of falling dead at the top. Yet he managed his autumn course of lectures. But he finally bowed to friendly pressure to abandon this cold and gloomy apartment, and he moved into ground floor rooms in Trinity Great Court, his friend Andrew Gow taking care of the move while he was in the Evelyn, even to the extent of supervising the transfer of his extensive library. For a while in these modernly-equipped rooms he was like a child (admittedly a very weak one) with a new toy, especially pleased with the bathroom (he was accustomed to a rather spartan hip-bath). He was full of gratitude for the kindnesses and solicitude of friends, displaying an openness of emotions quite uncharacteristic of him.

On 22 March 1936 he wrote to Houson Martin, one of a handful of American admirers of his poems, including the poet Witter Bynner, with whom he kept up a correspondence. The letter discourages Martin from publishing a book about him — "if you can restrain your indecent ardour for a little I shall be properly dead and your proposed work will not be by its nature unbecoming" (*P.&P.* p.472). He finished the letter with an explanation of his attitude to life:

In philosophy I am a Cyrenaic or egoistic hedonist, and regard the pleasure of the moment as the only possible motive of action. As for pessimism, I think it almost as silly, though not as wicked, as optimism. George Eliot said she was a meliorist: I am a pejorist, and also your sincerely . . . (*P.&P.* p.473)

Meliorism is the doctrine that the world may be made better by human effort. Presumably pejorism is the doctrine that it may be made worse. He had managed another term's lectures, but was back in the Evelyn. He was out again in the third week of April and gave two of the next term's lectures, but needed to sit down while doing so. April 24 saw his last lecture and his last meeting of the Family dining club, although he was too ill to eat. Next day he went back to the Evelyn where on 30 April 1936 he died peacefully.

At the service in Trinity College chapel Housman's own hymn 'For my Funeral' was sung (*MP* 47). There was a printing error in the sheet for the funeral service, which he would no doubt have considered inevitable, having spent most of his life in a losing battle against compositors. That is a story which still continues: the latest edition of the poems (*P.&P.*) includes the following gem in one of his most famous lines (*ASL* XL): "This is the land of lost content". In context the line is nonsense — "This" should be "That".

A.E. Housman's ashes lie beneath a stone tablet under the north wall of Ludlow Church, the same Ludlow Tower of his poems. A larger stone, set in the wall, quotes some of his own lines:

> Good-night; ensured release,
> Imperishable peace,
>   Have these for yours.

They come from 'Parta Quies' (*MP* XLVIII), a poem first published in his undergraduate years in the magazine *Waifs and Strays*.

Sexuality

In these days of clause 28/29 (the name is as elusive as what it is actually supposed to mean), when a photograph can be banned from a local authority art gallery merely for showing two adult males in the act of kissing, a lot of our past (recent and not so recent) is going to need careful consideration before it risks being revised out of all recognition. Perhaps if writers like Wilde, Auden and Housman were to be banned from schools, the literary prejudice of the British Isles would do some good for once. But it won't happen like that: certain works are being quietly dropped from the exam syllabuses. Certain ways of reading other texts will be 'discouraged', which is more subtle and therefore potentially more damaging.

We are being told that when two men, or two women, are committed to each other, when they set up a stable partnership, when they consider rearing children — something encouraged in certain U.S. states — any of this amounts to a "pretended family relationship". What is being denied to them is not sex but, as ever, love. There is heterosexual love and there are homosexual relationships. In the Aids debate heterosexuals have been assumed, in the end and against all the evidence, to be monogamous; homosexuals to be promiscuous.

Take a situation (one I have witnessed) where one person in a homosexual partnership of many years' standing dies. The surviving partner is bereaved, but there are constant social barriers erected against the public expression of this grief. In only very few cases will a church funeral service acknowledge the relationship. There is no homosexual equivalent to the words widow and widower, because there is in this country no way that two people of the same sex can publicly commit themselves to one another: no marriage for them, except in exceptional circumstances, which are

50

then not legally sanctioned. What has ended is now legally inscribed as a pretended family relationship, an imposture. In others words they have no family relationship.

I am not homosexual, and I only say that so that I will not be interpreted as writing out of self-interest. I make no apologies about expressing these opinions in a general book about another author, because they relate directly to my interpretation of that author. Nor do I apologise for including a whole chapter on the subject of Housman's homosexuality, since I am not the only Housman critic who believes the issue is central to the poetry. If it means that this book subtly fails to appear in secondary schools that might otherwise have bought it, or for that matter in libraries too, I do not think myself the irresponsible party.

★

> Any male person who, in public or private, commits, or is a party to the commission of, or procures or attempts to procure the commission by any male person of any act of gross indecency with another male person, shall be guilty of a misdemeanour, and being convicted thereof shall be liable at the discretion of the court to be imprisoned for any term not exceeding two years, with or without hard labour. (1885 Criminal Law Amendment Act, section 11: the 'Labouchère Amendment')

No aspect of Housman's work and life has caused as much comment and controversy as the question of his sexuality. Speculation is fuelled by the absence of almost any firm evidence on the issue, except for the following couple of facts. One is that Housman, a lifetime bachelor, developed in his undergraduate years a deep emotional attachment to the scientist and sportsman Moses Jackson, which seems to have remained unbroken throughout his life. The other is that certain, especially posthumous, poems refer to a failed or forbidden relationship in such a way as to strongly suggest an autobiographical basis, the relationship being clearly with another man. But the gist of the poems is what the relationship was *not*: i.e. reciprocated in its emotional intensity. Physical love, or passion, is never directly referred to in these poems. There is also one poem of 1895 (*AP* XVIII, 'Oh who is that young sinner with the handcuffs on his wrists?'), which clearly refers to the Wilde trials of that year and argues unequivocally that

51

Wilde was being imprisoned for something as little worthy of blame as the colour of his hair:

> 'Tis a shame to human nature, such a head of hair as his;
> In the good old time 'twas hanging for the colour that it is;
> Though hanging isn't bad enough and flaying would be fair
> For the nameless and abominable colour of his hair.

The word "nameless" refers directly to Wilde's speech in his own defence: the famous phrase, "the love that dare not speak its name". To understand the importance of these words and of the Wilde trials themselves, and to put the whole question of Housman's homosexuality into a historical perspective, I will have to make a digression into the relationship between Victorian society and sexuality.

Firstly, the word. In some ways Housman gets it right more than Wilde here, since "nameless" is perhaps the true situation of homosexuality at this time. The two non-pejorative terms for sexual relations between partners of the same sex, 'homosexuality' and 'inversion', both entered the English language during the 1890s, both in the realm of medical speculation. The former was coined in 1869 by the Swiss doctor Karoly Maria Benkert and was introduced into English by Havelock Ellis, the sexologist. 'Inversion' was the term favoured by the psychoanalyst Sigmund Freud. It is unlikely that either of these words had any popular currency at the time of the Wilde trials. In fact it was only in 1885, with the infamous 'Labouchère Amendment' (quoted above) that the law first recognized male homosexuality as a specific crime. Before this time, homosexual practices had been punishable under the catch-all offence of sodomy. This crime could cover any forms of sexual activity that did not have conception as their ultimate aim — anything from bestiality to birth control. These were seen as essentially crimes "against nature", and punishment was severe, the death penalty only having been tacitly dropped for them in 1836 and finally abolished in 1861, hence Housman's "good old time". As an instance of this severity when guilt was proven, which was technically not always easy, in 1810, four out of five convicted sodomists were hanged, as opposed to 471 out of 613 for other capital offences.

In 1826 Sir Robert Peel not only made the technicalities of proof easier for the prosecution, but re-enacted the death penalty at the same time as it was dropped for a hundred other offences. Amongst all this lesbanism, because the social condition of women rendered it virtually invisible, was never mentioned or recognized. Women's sexuality was controlled through the laws against prostitution, typified by the 1864 Contagious Diseases Act, designed to prevent infection amongst the armed services:

> This bill meant that any woman who was said to be a prostitute could be forcibly examined and imprisoned if she resisted. If she had VD she could be kept in the 'Lock Hospital' for three months. There was no compulsion on men to be treated for VD. Instead of being innocent until proved guilty, the women were defined as guilty and had to prove their innocence. (Sheila Rowbotham, *Hidden from History*, London, Pluto Press, 1977, p.52).

This helps to show the extent of Victorian legislative intrusion on women's private lives. The work of Henry Labouchère in extending this to all male homosexual practices and contacts, and its use of the word 'procurement' from the terminology of prostitution, helped to create the image of the homosexual as engaging in clandestine and nefarious liaisons, and at the same time guaranteed that such behaviour was necessitated. Similarly it heightened awareness of male prostitutes or 'mary-anns'. The Cleveland Street scandal of 1889–90 involving a homosexual brothel, 'telegraph boys' and several prominent figures, gave the issue a public airing, as a government attempt at a cover-up basically backfired. Then came the Wilde affair.

As is well known, this began when the Marquis of Queensberry publicly and illiterately accused Wilde of "posing as a Somdomite [sic]". Wilde attempted a disastrous libel suit, which led to the three trials of his own conduct and character. It is as well to note now what Jeffrey Weeks has to say about his testimony:

> Oscar Wilde's famous defence of the "Love that dare not speak its name" was a defence of "that deep, spiritual affection that is as pure as it is perfect" rather than of the sexual life he actually led (*CO* p.43),

which was characterised by prostitution, predominantly with

youths. In fact, corruption of youth was one of the major aspects of such scandals and, since it threatened the basis of family life in the eyes of social purity campaigners so influential at the time, was responsible for much of the depth of feeling against all homosexuals.

Havelock Ellis, in volume two of his *Studies in the Psychology of Sex*, claimed that the trials helped to make homosexuals aware of themselves as a social group, and it seems certain that this is true. It is from about this time that the earliest support and pressure groups for homosexuals and those interested in sexual freedom begin to emerge. One of these, the Order of Chaeronia, had Laurence Housman as one of its founder members. It was a secret society, taking its name from the battle of Chaeronia, in which Philip of Macedon's army defeated the Athenians. Fighting on the Athenian side was a band of three hundred Thebans, a strike force bound together by ties of loyalty and love. Heavily outnumbered they fought and died, earning this tribute from Philip of Macedon: "Perish any man who suspects that these men either did or suffered anything that was base". This group of soldiers became, for some late nineteenth century homosexuals, an emblem of their newly-emerging cause. Weeks is undoubtedly wrong to suggest that A.E. Housman may have been a member of the Order; if he were, it is unlikely that Laurence, in *De Amicitia*, should make it clear that he only suspected the truth about his brother's sexuality. Also Housman engaged in little direct political action, after a brief flurry of Tory enthusiasm soon after arriving in Oxford. After that, the nearest to political activism he got was probably to donate his bank balance to the Exchequer at the start of World War One. Added to this is the very fact of his conservatism, his general disapproval of all Laurence's political allegiances — with the peace movement and the suffragettes — although here his words may seem harder than his actual feelings, just as he is known to have said kinder things about his brother's poetry than he ever expressed to his face or in letters. One interesting piece of evidence in this respect, and one that provides highlight to the issue of his misogyny, is a meeting of the U.C.L. Debating Society in October 1892, during which Housman was in the chair. The motion was "That this house does not approve of the extension of the franchise to women". There were twelve members present and the motion was defeated by seven votes to six. This suggests that Housman exercised the casting vote against the motion. This is another of those occasional incidents that suggest he was not as intolerant as he liked people to think.

Most of the members of the Order of Chaeronia were, like leading light Gilbert Ives, socialists of one kind or another. Two things seem to characterise homosexual politics in the late nineteenth and early twentieth centuries. These were socialism, and support for the women's suffrage movement, in the latter of which Laurence and Clemence Housman became quite prominent, Clemence at one time spending a week in Holloway prison for refusing to pay taxes in protest. Despite what I have just said about his possible exaggerations of his opinions, it is still unthinkable that their brother would go out of his way to be involved in a secret society populated entirely by political radicals. Men associated with the Order were, quite obviously, practising homosexuals: we do not know as much of A.E.H.

While Laurence went on to become chairman of the British Society for the Study of Sex Psychology (which in the 1920s became the British Sexological Society) none of Alfred's writings, public or private, suggest that he was aware of the fight for the reform of the law and of social attitudes with regard to sexuality. But his attitudes can to some extent be distilled from aspects of his life and work, and though this may lead us too close to biographical speculation for comfort, it seems to be one way of seeing A.E. Housman in perspective.

The clearest evidence comes in the form of the poem about Oscar Wilde, a poem which he chose naturally not to publish during his own lifetime but which Laurence was sure he intended him to make public after his death. It clearly presents a case for homosexuality as an inborn characteristic, one not in itself sinful or pathological but offensive to the moral judgements of the time:

> Oh a deal of pains he's taken and a pretty price he's paid
> To hide his poll or dye it of a mentionable shade;
> But they've pulled the beggar's hat off for the world to
>   see and stare,
> And they're haling him to justice for the colour of his hair.

Inherent in the metaphor is the assumption that homosexuality is nothing but a simple variation. Nor can it be treated, like a disease, but can only be disguised, covered over, secreted. Wilde's sexuality is seen as something beyond his own choice, and he is therefore being punished unreasonably; but justice, as so often in Housman's poems, takes no account of such contingent matters.

Another poem, *ASL* XLIV ('Shot? so quick, so clean an ending?') has a particular history of its own. After his brother's death, Laurence found, in his personal copy of *A Shropshire Lad*, a newspaper clipping marking the page of this poem. It referred to the death of a young Woolwich Cadet who had committed suicide on 6 August 1895, leaving a letter explaining his action, from which the passage relevant to the poem runs as follows:

> I wish it to be clearly understood that I am not what is commonly called 'temporarily insane', and that I am putting an end to my life after several weeks of careful deliberation. I do not think that I need justify my actions to anyone but my Maker, but . . . I will state the main reasons which have determined me. The first is utter cowardice and despair. There is only one thing in this world which would make me thoroughly happy; that one thing I have no earthly hope of obtaining. The second — which I wish was the only one — is that I have absolutely ruined my own life; but I thank God that as yet, so far as I know, I have not morally injured, or 'offended', as it is called in the Bible, anyone else. Now I am quite certain that I could not live another five years without doing so, and for that reason alone, even if the first did not exist, I should do what I am doing . . . At all events it is final, and consequently better than a long series of sorrows and disgraces. (*P.&P.* p.483)

He was killing himself in despair over his homosexual condition, just over two months after Wilde's conviction. Housman's poem, a literal memorial to his death although it never mentions the man's troubles directly (neither, for that matter, does the Wilde poem), again paints the picture of a suffering before which the sufferer is powerless, except to do what in the end he did do: "Yours was not an ill for mending,/'Twas best to take it to the grave". It is something incurable again, but this time something which renders life genuinely shameful, even worthless:

> Oh soon, and better so than later
> After long disgrace and scorn,

> You shot dead the household traitor,
> The soul that should not have been born.

It may be worth reading the last line of the stanza again, and then to compare it with Wilde's "the love that dare not speak its name". In terms of rhythm, syntax and cadence they are so near to being identical that it is surely more than coincidence, coming as close to each other historically as the two phrases do. At the very least it is an unconscious echo; either way it is an inherently ironic one. "The love that dare not speak its name" is a defence; "The soul that should not have been born" is utter condemnation.

Like many another of Housman's soldiers, the meaning of life for the Cadet is in a good death, and as they die on the battlefield defending their fellows against the enemy, he dies defending them from himself:

> Souls undone, undoing others,—
> Long time since the tale began.
> You would not live to wrong your brothers:
> Oh lad, you died as fits a man.

Dying for one's fellow men is such a keynote in the poems, and not only those with military subjects, that it is worth asking what this may have to do with the homosexual question. Having raised that question I want to leave it fallow until the next chapter and a discussion of the role of death in Housman's work. What occupies me more now is the strange contradictory relationship between the two poems we have been looking at.

Wilde is presented as the victim of prejudice and injustice, but the Cadet metes out the ultimate penalty on himself and is complimented for it. Yet he had not 'offended' anybody and Wilde, in that sense, had. Is poetic justice being a bit hard on the more 'innocent' party, even given that it is himself as well as others that he is saving from disgrace? There are, I think, three possible explanations which need to be considered. The first is that Housman experienced this contradiction within himself; that he felt an extreme ambivalence with regard to his sexuality, making it equally possible for him to feel sympathy with the plight of Wilde while, in another mood, he could envy the resolve of the Woolwich Cadet. Hence the stanza:

> Now to your grave shall friend and stranger
>   With ruth and some with envy come:
> Undishonoured, clear of danger,
>   Clean of guilt, pass hence and home.

The second explanation relates closely to the first. It relates to Housman's tendency — as illustrated by his misogyny — to act and talk in quite contradictory ways. So he always cast scorn on the suffrage movement in public and family circles but appears, in the more impersonal context of chairing a debating society, to have quietly voted in their favour. In the present case one poem, with its more socially acceptable moral, was chosen for public consumption; the other was held back until he was himself "clear of danger". This does not mean that either his misogyny or his approval of the Woolwich Cadet's death were merely masks or impostures: they may simply have belonged quite naturally to different aspects of his personality. I do not mean to suggest that Housman was in any way schizophrenic: one can understand the nature of internal contradictions in a person's character without having to resort to imputing a pathological dissociation of the emotions or the intellect. They are common to us all, particularly in areas which cause the most personal stress; like sexuality.

The third explanation may be seen as building on and complementing the other two. *Last Poems* XII is a discursive piece, railing against 'These foreign laws of God and man.' It is written from the standpoint of

> I, a stranger and afraid
> In a world I never made

and hedged around with hypocritical restrictions:

> . . . let God and man decree
> Laws for themselves and not for me;
> And if my ways are not as theirs
> Let them mind their own affairs.
> Their deeds I judge and much condemn,
> Yet when did I make laws for them?

The poem straightforwardly represents a kind of amoral — as opposed to immoral — viewpoint. It is a viewpoint which, as we shall see in the next chapter, the poems are continually opening up for interrogation. The figures of the condemned criminal, the deserter, the murderer, all seem to be implicitly asking the question, 'What is moral?' and 'Whose morality is this?' I take it as being a question which goes beyond any biographical considerations, although it would obviously relate to Housman finding his sexuality and his ideas of love in conflict with the morality of his age. But it also relates to the problem of forging a moral consciousness in the absence of religious belief; and not only a moral consciousness, but the very morals upon which it is to be built. *LP* XII exhibits the struggle with an inherited moral code which, though it is based upon a religion the poem's speaker no longer has any faith in, and though it offends his sense of what morality should be, is nevertheless the only morality there is to live by:

> They will be master, right or wrong;
> Though both are foolish, both are strong.
> And since, my soul, we cannot fly
> To Saturn nor to Mercury,
> Keep we must, if keep we can,
> These foreign laws of God and man.

The choice of planets here is significant: Saturn is identified with the Greek god Kronos, ruler of the world in the golden age of innocence. Mercury, of course, is not only the messenger to the gods, but the Roman god of thieves: they stand at opposite ends of the moral spectrum, one beyond the need for morality, the other beyond its enforcement. Both are free, but all human reality lies between these poles. I want to prise this aspect of Housman's work away from biographical considerations, because, as I hope the first chapter has shown, he was a very moral, and morally conventional, man in his day to day life, and none of this interrogation of morality which appears in the poems ever expressed itself politically, or even personally in the pages of his letters. In terms of his actual lived experience, then, the key line of the poem would seem to be, "Keep we must, if keep we can". But the poems work on a different level to this, for reasons upon which it is, I think, permissible to speculate, but with effects that express themselves in the texture of the poems.

I want to suggest that the struggle with conventional morality presented in clear terms in *LP* XII underpins the apparent contradictions between, and within, other Housman poems. It is a context in which both Wilde and the Woolwich Cadet can be seen as exemplary figures: one representing the impossible attempt to express one's own inner needs secretly, within the contradicting morality, to 'disguise' oneself; the other accepting the inevitability of the existing system, and the fact that it provides the basis of truth, honour and shame for the people living within that system, and therefore putting himself beyond it in the only way really open to him by killing himself. The one remains true to himself, the other to the people around him. It all comes back to the line we have just looked at in the later poem, 'The laws of God the laws of man': "Keep we must, if keep we can". If we can't, we can either break them, or die: Mercury, the transgression of the law; or Saturn, the innocence beyond it we can only find in death, which for Housman the atheist, would take us beyond man *and* God. These two poems of 1895 represent the two ways of absolute rejection, or of the inability to accept, the given moral code. Everything else is struggle and compromise in the attempt to lead a moral life between the twin dangers of crime and death.

Now I want to return to the question of Victorian notions of homosexuality. These emerged almost exclusively from medical science (the one arena where the issue could be openly discussed and written about) and tend therefore to see homosexuality as a problem of pathology. Two main theories emerge from this debate, focusing on the origin of the 'condition' rather than its effects. Homosexuality is either congenital, or acquired via the influence of one's society or environment. The congenital theory of homosexuality tended to be the focus of the early sex-reformers in the wake of the Wilde affair, since it promised to put an end to the belief that the homosexual is a criminal. They thought to establish that inversion was an innate but essentially harmless characteristic, rather like the colour of a person's hair, in fact. The negative side of this theory is that it could also be used as a theory of madness. If you assumed that this was indeed a harmful condition, either to the 'sufferer' or to those around him, then its incurability would lead him directly to the asylum.

The theory that homosexuality was an acquired condition is more in line with modern ideas about the flexibility of sexuality in response to social conditioning. But in late nineteenth century

England this theory was too closely allied to the notion underlying the sodomy laws of a crime 'against nature'. In this sense it was still something to be punished. More often, as time went on, it was this theory that underpinned the widespread belief that homosexuals be treated for their 'illness', and that, since acquired in the first place, it could in some way be cured. Many homosexuals were in fact convinced themselves that they were ill. The Irish patriot Sir Roger Casement was one of these, and Goldsworthy Lowes Dickinson, the liberal humanist, said that he was like a "man born crippled". Treatment (if such a word can be used) for homosexuality continued to be prescribed into the 1960s and included cold showers, marriage, hypnotism, chemical experiments and aversion therapy. In this sense it is a particularly twentieth century theory, and it is not surprising that with regard to Housman we can ignore it completely. But there is one interesting sidelight to this. Wilde in his petition for a reduction of sentence claimed to have been suffering from 'erotomania' leading to temporary mental collapse.

In a sense, as I have already suggested, Wilde was the first positive role model for English homosexuals. It is true that many felt a strong identification with sexual mores of the ancient Greeks and no doubt the strong interest which many had in youths was connected with Hellenist views of male beauty. But it was up to the reform societies to attempt to create the social being we now understand as the homosexual person. It is hard to think back to that time, to imagine belonging then to what we only now understand as a complete sexual identity. That identity was then totally bound up with notions of criminality and illness, and books discussing the subject were banned unless aimed specifically at a medical readership. This is what happened to the second volume of Havelock Ellis's *Studies in the Psychology of Sex* entitled *Sexual Inversion*. This book was published in 1897 by the Legitimation League, a society dedicated to sex reform but under suspicion from the police of having connections with anarchism. Its secretary George Bedborough was put on trial for selling *Sexual Inversion* and persuaded to plead guilty, thus allowing the authorities to ban the book without its merits or demerits ever coming to trial. It was an honest and scientific investigation, but aimed at a more general audience than those in the medical profession, which was its real cause of offence. Ellis's reaction to this example of British justice was to decide to publish no more volumes of his *Studies* in Britain. It was against this kind of treatment that homosexuals had to build what defences they could, forging alliances, as Edward Carpenter did with socialism and Laurence Housman with feminism, and building up a more and more sophisticated picture of the homosexual nature, going as far as Carpenter's notion — not entirely free in its formulation from implications of some inborn disorder — of an 'intermediate sex'. It is in this context that we must read what we can gather about A.E. Housman's sexuality.

The first printed hint at his homosexuality was made by Laurence in his *A.E.H.* In *More Poems* he had already published some of the poems which relate to Moses Jackson (*MP* XII, XXIII, XXX & XXXI), and in *Additional Poems* he printed others, and the Wilde poem, which he felt the need to explain including: " . . . I feel quite sure that though it is not of a high standard it says something which A.E.H. very much wished to say, but perhaps preferred not to say in his own lifetime" (*A.E.H.* p.213). This hint was not seriously taken up until the first full-length biographies appeared in the late 1950s, those by George L. Watson (1957) and Maude Hawkins (1958). Neither is as concerned as they might be with reliance upon fact above speculation however, and they lacked the one major piece of evidence, which did not appear for another decade. It was in 1967 that John Carter published Laurence's *A.E. Housman's "De Amicitia"* in the October issue of *Encounter*. This is an account of Alfred's relationship with Moses Jackson as known by Laurence, written around 1942, when it was placed in a sealed envelope in the British Museum to be opened after twenty-five years.

Laurence only met Jackson once or twice but, besides clues in the poems, letters and the memories of friends, he had Housman's diaries for the years 1888, 1889, 1890 and 1891 (which contains only one entry, for the year 1898). Most of the material in these diaries consists of Housman's brief but meticulous observations of the changing seasons, the first appearance of flowers and blossoms, etc. The other terse entries refer directly or indirectly to Moses Jackson, and these Laurence prints in full. They are not very revealing. They begin after Jackson's departure for India on the 'Bokhara' and follow its voyage and that of the 'Mongolia' Moses transferred to at Suez. They are one-line notes of departure and arrival, punctuated by a mention of meeting 'Add' (Adalbert Jackson) for lunch. Moses is referred to consistently as 'he', other people like Adalbert and colleagues at the Office by some kind of shorthand. He notes the arrival of letters from Moses as well as the sending of others to him. Significantly it appears that his first letter from India was to another employee at the Patent Office, Nightingale, and not Alfred. The next year's diary (1889) notes some details of Jackson's visit to England, when he appears to have met Housman only twice, briefly. The most significant entry again implies an omission. On January 7, 1890, three weeks after Moses left England (on the day after his wedding) occur the words "I heard he was married". It appears that Housman stopped keeping a diary in 1890, but the one entry in the 1891 diary refers to May 22 of a later year and reads: "Sunday 1898, 10.45 p.m. said goodbye". They were to meet again a few years later, on a fairly jocular occasion by all accounts, when they stayed with Arthur Pollard and it seems regressed to undergraduate behaviour.

Laurence understandably interprets these entries as proof of Alfred's deep love for Jackson. Equally significant is the fact that a man who had seen to the destruction of most of his personal papers, had left these diaries to be dealt with at his brother's discretion. Once in later life, explaining that a portrait of a middle-aged man hanging over his fireplace was Jackson, Alfred told Laurence that Jackson was "the man who had more influence on my life than anyone else". This admission apparently struck Laurence at the time as very surprising. He had of course known almost nothing about Alfred's private life during the London years. In addition to this Laurence also mentions obscurely the presence among Housman's papers of material indicating his preferences concerning the human form, material now, of course, destroyed in accordance with Housman's will. As Housman's literary executor Laurence had the responsibility of destroying not only his private papers and unpublished prose, but also any poems and fragments of poems that were not of a standard equal to those he himself published, or working drafts for those poems. Laurence decided to preserve the workings drafts of poems already published. The result in terms of the notebooks in which Housman wrote his poems, was to produce a series of virtual scrapbooks — pages and fragments of pages glued down on folio sheets with lines scored out here and there. A nightmare no doubt for the poet's brother to have to do, and a nightmare for anybody trying to piece together the genesis of the poems. These notebook fragments are now preserved in the Library of Congress in America, the mounting sheets removed to aid conservation, revealing material never meant to be seen. But again, this material does not seem to tell us much more about Housman than we already knew, although no full collation of the manuscripts has been published.

We keep returning to how little we know. It is the very paucity of the available evidence which has fuelled such speculations as those of Richard Graves, whose ideas I will come to soon. Not only are there so many gaps that beg to be filled in with something (sometimes anything), but the nature of Housman's secretiveness about his private life raises questions which are difficult to ignore. So, many theories have sprung up about the incident in 1885 when he disappeared for a week after what seems to have been some kind of scene or argument with Jackson. It is possible — only possible — that this split may have been caused by Jackson's meeting Laurence and Clemence, either at an exhibition or at the house of a mutual aquaintance, a meeting at which Alfred was probably not present. All that is known of the meeting is that Jackson was surprised to learn that Alfred had a brother and sister staying in London (they had been there since the summer of 1884, writing and studying art). Alfred had never invited them to visit his lodgings (he was similarly inhospitable while living on his own in Byron Cottage), though he certainly used to call on them. It would be quite natural for Moses to be somewhat put out at being kept in the dark this way, and of also being kept as a secret himself. It only remains for us to ask how much this secretiveness had to do with Housman's feelings for his friend, and how much these fuelled the event into a crisis — leading to his leaving the shared lodgings for good — and then to leave it at that: open, a possibility. Graves makes a confident case for the crisis being precipitated by Alfred's realization that his feelings for Jackson would never be reciprocated. About time too after half a dozen years, you might say, since it does seem rather a long time to wait for a 'loves me, loves me not' crisis. But the real problem here is the evidence Graves uses to back it up.

1. Sarah Jane Housman

2. Edward Housman as a Young Man

3. Perry Hall, Bromsgrove

4. Fockbury House

5. A.E. Housman at Eighteen

6. The Young Moses Jackson

7. A.E. Housman at Thirty-Five

8. Ludlow Tower

9. Hughley Steeple

I.

1887

From Clee to heaven the beacon burns,
The shires have seen it plain,
From north and south the sign returns
And beacons burn again.

Look left, look right, the hills are bright,
The dales are light between,
Because 'tis fifty years tonight
That God has saved the Queen.

Now, when the flame they watch not towers
About the soil they trod,
Lads, we'll remember friends of ours
Who shared the work with God.

To skies that knit their heartstrings right,
To fields that bred them brave,
The saviours come not home tonight:
Themselves they could not save.

It dawns in Asia, tombstones show
And Shropshire names are read;
And the Nile spills his overflow
Beside the Severn's dead.

We pledge in peace by farm and town
The Queen they served in war,
And fire the beacons up and down
The land they perished for.

'God save the Queen' we living sing,
From height to height 'tis heard;
And with the rest your voices ring,
Lads of the Fifty-third.

Oh, God will save her, fear you not:
Be you the men you've been,
Get you the sons your fathers got,
And God will save the Queen.

10. Autograph of '1887'

11. Laurence Housman

13. A.E. Housman in Old Age

12. A.E. Housman in Relaxed Fashion

Again without any provisos, Graves says that *MP* XXI, a poem ending with the stanza,

Oh worse remains for others
And worse to fear had I
Than so at four-and-twenty
To lay me down and die

though written later, refers to this "unhappy time" (Graves p.65). He does mention that Housman was in fact twenty-six at this time, but excuses himself by saying that the age had gone through at least one change for the sake of the sound of the poem. Not having seen the manuscript myself I do not know what it was changed from, but somehow suspect that if it was twenty-six Graves would have said so. I guess this kind of evidence might have gone down well in a Victorian court trying a homosexual; but it won't do for me. We do not know *for sure* that Jackson ever knew the full extent of his friend's feelings for him, though we might expect that he almost certainly had an idea. We do not even know *for sure* that the relationship between them was not at some time physically consummated, though we can be almost certain that it wasn't. The evidence of the poems we *presume* to be autobiographical is of a great feeling of love on one side which was simply not reciprocated on the other. Whatever the expressions of dejection and despair there are no accusations that the other party was actively cruel or hurtful; nor are the poems in any way erotic, though a suppressed, unconscious eroticism could be read into other poems not concerned with this relationship. It would be an insult to the thoroughness with which Housman hid his inner feelings and covered his tracks to make any confident assertions with regard to his sex life. As a textual critic he was a master at filling the gaps and distortions in texts: he was just as skilful at creating them.

Another area of similar speculation is Jackson's failure to inform Housman about his wedding until after he had left the country. The Graves hypothesis is that he was trying to spare his feelings. But another theory stems from the very apparent cooling of their relationship after Alfred left the house in Bayswater. It chimes in with Nightingale receiving the first letter back from India, and with them apparently only meeting twice during Jackson's 1889 visit. Far from being a blow to Housman, it appears that they actually got on rather better after the wedding, both during Jackson's visits and via correspondence.

I don't want to get bogged down in another Graves-churned mud-bath, the question of a physical relationship having taken place between Adalbert Jackson and Housman after Moses left for India. It all stems from a series of assertions made by Laurence Housman in letters to Maude Hawkins that Adalbert had reciprocated affection from Alfred. These letters were written in 1958 when Laurence was in his nineties and his memory, by his own admission five years before, was "a wreck". They are based on evidence we will never see, if on any evidence at all. Laurence doesn't say if there was anything in the destroyed private papers to prove it, and for the most part the phrases quoted by Carter in *De Amicitia* from these letters carry more belief than conviction. But there is just a possibility. All we do know is they were good friends, that Housman wrote *MP* XLII and probably *MP* XLI about him, and that his photograph hung in Housman's rooms beside that of his brother.

There is still one more biographical shot-in-the-dark to mention. There is a piece of card, written in Housman's hand, which consists of three columns. The one on the left is a series of days of the week, complete from Monday to a week the following Monday. The next column is numbers, one for each day, being either 9, 0, 3, or 10. The last, it seems, is either a name or the name of a profession or type of person: e.g. Max, Danseur, nègre, and this column is blank when there is a zero in the first column. Written from bottom to top in the right-hand margin is the comment "10 in 15 days". It has been said that these notes bear some resemblance to those made by Roger Casement in his homosexual diaries, and Graves (again) confidently interprets them as recording contacts with homosexual prostitutes in Paris. P.G. Naiditch has dealt with this theory in an admirable article in the *Housman Society Journal* (1986, pp. 55–70). He throws a great deal of doubt on this interpretation in a very thorough consideration, of which I will summarise the main points. Evidence shows that the document can be dated to a visit Housman paid to Paris in 1932 when he was seventy-three. Ten contacts in fifteen days in the year before his health started to deteriorate sounds like a remarkable piece of promiscuity. If the numbers are prices, things just don't seem to add up. If he's listing them in francs, as one would expect him to, then a male prostitute could be got for as little as the cost of two postage stamps. If on the other hand the numbers represent pounds sterling, then the ten contacts cost him as much as a sixty day stay at the expensive Continental Hotel in Paris. It has been suggested that the numbers represent marks awarded out of ten to these prostitutes; but why only the figures 9, 3 and 10? Also, in either of the above cases, why write '0' instead of '-' when no contact was made?

Naiditch points out that there was a restaurant called Marins and a Tav du Nègre in the city at that time, but discounts the possibility in this context due to Housman's inconsistency in capitalisations in the list, and the fact that the numbers 1 and 2 follow the two instances of Marin in the list as well as a two after the second "danseur". However, there is a second piece of identical card with another list which clearly refers to Housman's eating habits on the same trip, although it is impossible to say how the two may relate to each other. Another theory, also somewhat unlikely, suggests that the list in question relates to the sexual exploits of some friend or companion of Housman's. He is known to have sometimes been accompanied by unidentified people whilst abroad, who were almost certainly not chauffeurs; he once warned Grant Richards off meeting him because he thought he would not mix with the friend he had with him. Other than this nothing is really known about this friend or friends; but the theory only disposes of the problem of Housman's age, not the other objections. Perhaps the numbers refer to the times of the contacts, but three o'clock, morning or afternoon, would surely be an unlikely time.

I have one further, open-ended observation to add to those made by Naiditch. There seems to be some kind of sequence in the numbers. 0 appears next to the Saturdays and Wednesdays only, with the exception of the second of the three Mondays. 3 is allocated to the two Thursdays and two Sundays only. The other days have a 9, except for the last Friday and the last Monday, which have 10, so that no 9s appear after the first 10. Although this doesn't amount to a consistent sequence, it seems to me to be too close to be coincidental. What it may mean I have no idea. I could almost accuse Housman of mischievously planting the thing, just to confound the investigations of biographers.

Andrea, the young Venetian Housman referred to as "my

gondolier", has been another cause of speculation. Housman met and befriended Andrea on his first visit to Venice in 1900 when the young man was twenty-three. Until 1908 Alfred made regular visits to Venice and always employed Andrea. After that he had one more fleeting glimpse of the city in 1912, but his frequent holidays there had finished. But when, in 1926, a message came from Andrea that he was dying, Housman rushed off to see him, finding him somewhat less ill than expected. But Andrea remained ill and was supported to some extent by regular gifts of money from his friend — he had, as I have said, a large extended family to look after. Andrea died in 1930, after which his family pestered Housman with begging letters, much to his annoyance. He sent no more money.

These are the basic facts of the matter; that there is a case for a possible sexual relationship between the two men is undeniable, but we can have no confidence in drawing such a conclusion. Liaisons with gondoliers were not unknown to English homosexuals — John Addington Symonds had such a lover — and the way Housman rushed across Europe to the bedside of a man he had not seen for fourteen years or so certainly shows that whatever his feelings were for Andrea, they obviously remained quite strong. Graves interprets Housman's sudden loss of interest in Venice in 1908 as being due to a rift between the two men. His evidence for this rests solely on a poem, *MP* XLIV ('Far known to sea and shore'), about the rebuilding of the Campanile. The last stanza is the crucial one:

> It looks to north and south,
>   It looks to east and west;
> It guides to Lido mouth
>   The steersman of Triest.
>
>   Andrea, fare you well;
>   Venice, farewell to thee.
>   The tower that stood and fell
>   Is not rebuilt in me.

Graves's interpretation rests on what seems, in the context of modern critical practice, to be a fairly obvious phallic image in the final two lines. It is difficult to ignore it in reading the poem. Whether Housman meant it or not, it is there: but that is just the point — did Housman mean it? As Norman Page says, "there are times when a tower is just a tower" (*Page* p.123), and it was certainly not Housman's practice to weight poems with such blatant sexual metaphors. I will have more to say about the ways in which sexuality expressed itself unconsciously in his work: even in that context this is a singular example of a representation of the phallus. It may just be, as Page suggests, a coincidence, something that merely looks like a sexual image. And even it if isn't, even if Freud was right to believe that in the workings of the human mind there is no such thing as coincidence, nevertheless the fact that one man produces, consciously or unconsciously, a sexual metaphor in relation to another man he knew well, does not mean they actually had a love-affair. I say this knowing full well that I may sound a little naive, for there are other motives which may have led Housman to befriend Andrea as he did, and one of those is pity. The gondolier may have cut a pretty sorry figure for Housman: one-eyed, young, struggling to support a houseful of relatives. The normally stand-offish professor could respond very generously to people who were the victims of hardship or personal tragedy, as when his cousin Jerry lost an arm duing the Great War and Housman offered to pick up the bill for the best artificial arm available. I don't say that they didn't have some kind of love affair; I don't even say that I don't personally *believe* they did: I don't know what to believe, and it is best to admit it. There is a Housman uncertainty principle: it sets up a set of circumstances that strongly suggest a certain conclusion, but denies you anything like proof.

There is a poem (*MP* XXII) which has been taken as proof that, one way or another, Housman did experience the joys of human love. It begins:

> Ho, everyone that thirsteth
>   And hath the price to give,
> Come to the stolen waters,
>   Drink and your soul shall live.

Laurence was happy to think that, after his unhappy attachment to Moses Jackson, his brother did receive some love. We can make up our own story — Adalbert Jackson, homosexual prostitutes, Andrea: any or all of these — but it is unlikely to be Housman's story. If he did taste the "stolen waters" we don't know what they were, nor the complex of emotions with which he drank them. Too many people have played the 'did he/didn't he?' game that we're all in danger of losing sight of what he did do. He wrote.

II

The Writer

Shropshire

Housman's popular reputation as a poet is unusual in that it is based so much upon a single collection of short lyrics, *A Shropshire Lad*. It is possible that more people know the title of this book than know the name of its author; but how many could tell you the title of one of Thomas Hardy's original volumes, and how many slim volumes of verse from the late nineteenth century are still available, under separate covers, having never gone out of print? The phenomenon takes some explaining. How much is it due to the unity of the volume and its presentation of the world of Housman's Shropshire? How much might it be due to its author's own refusal, for the forty years he lived after its publication, to have it printed as anything but a separate volume? It might even have something to do with the title, suggested by Arthur Pollard to replace the rather less memorable *Poems by Terence Hearsay*. Perhaps the matter will become a little clearer if we look at two almost inseparable subjects — the poet's Shropshire, and Shropshire's poet.

The first thing to say about Housman's Shropshire is that it is not, and never was, the county on the Welsh border normally represented by that name. In fact it is as mythical as the Britain of Tennyson's *Idylls of the King*, or the pastoral setting of Sir Philip Sidney's *Arcadia*. It is not that the poet did not know Shropshire well, having never lived there, though he didn't; it is not even that he falsified the geography of the place to suit himself, though he did: it is more that in creating Shropshire he produced a stage, a little world on which to set in motion the characters, the emotions and the dramas that he needed to portray. What he produced is therefore much closer to Tolkien's Middle Earth, than the historically-rooted accuracy of Hardy's Wessex.

73

Housman's involvement with Shropshire began, probably, during the years of his family's occupation of Fockbury House:

> One of his pleasures was to reach some point where he could see extensive views. There was one hill quite close to The Clock House, in a field at the top of Worms Ash Lane, that gave him this with little trouble. We called the place 'Mount Pisgah.'
> (Kate Symons in *Brom*, pp.12–15)

The Canaan behind which Housman would see the sun set from this view-point was the South Shropshire hill country. The adolescent, who in a few years would fall in love with a young man called Moses, would spend evenings looking across to what he eventually called "the land of lost content" (*ASL* XL). That Alfred did visit Shropshire is known. He knew Ludlow and Bridgnorth; he had, I believe, been to Shrewsbury. He had travelled amongst at least some of the Shropshire hills, the Clees, Wenlock Edge, the Wrekin — those which lie closest to his native Worcestershire. And in the poems he keeps very much to this southern and eastern quarter of the county which he knew. Some of the most beautiful and well-known scenery in the county surrounds the Long Mynd and the tumbled outcrops of the Stiperstones; but these are out in the west of the major north-south valley which connects Ludlow with Shrewsbury to the north, and they are never even mentioned in *A Shropshire Lad*.

Housman mapped out his territory in a 1935 letter to his American admirer Houston Martin:

> I am Worcestershire by birth: Shropshire was our western horizon, which made me feel romantic about it. I do not know the county well, except in parts, and some of my topographical details are wrong and imaginary. The Wrekin is wooded, and Wenlock Edge along the western side, but the Clees and most of the other hills are grass or heather. In the southern half of the county, to which I have confined myself, the hills are generally long ridges running from north to south, with valleys, broad or narrow, between. The northern half is part of the great Cheshire plain. The Wrekin is isolated . . . . (*Letters*, p.352)

To be more specific about the boundaries of Housman's Shropshire; if you take the long escarpment of Wenlock Edge, running north-west from Craven Arms to Much Wenlock, everything south and east of this line is included, as is the very south-west corner of the country around Clun and down to Knighton (which is actually the wrong side of the River Teme to be in Shropshire and was then in Radnorshire in Wales, a county now subsumed under Powys). Taking the line north from Much Wenlock brings you to the Wrekin, the real northern outcrop of the Shropshire Lad's territory. Shrewsbury, the county town, lies about eight miles west of the Wrekin, and though it is mentioned in three poems in *A Shropshire Lad*, it is not really part of the landscape of the poems, whose true capital is Ludlow.

I have said that Housman's Shropshire is not the geographical county, and yet the fact that one can map it so clearly suggests otherwise. Even his own claim about details being "wrong and imaginary" needs to be looked at. Of course, in one quite well-known case they were. I quote again from Laurence's *A.E.H.*:

> It happened that, in the same year when *A Shropshire Lad* was published, I went to stay with friends at Buildwas; and finding that Hughley and its steeple were only five miles away, I walked over to have a look at the 'far-known sign' and the graves of suicides on north side of the tower. When I reached it, I found that the 'far-known sign' was buried away in a valley, and that the suicides were most of them respectable church-wardens and wives of vicars, all in neatly- tended graves. (p. 82)

Alfred had substituted Hughley for a place with an ugly name: "I did not apprehend," he wrote to Laurence, "that the faithful would be making pilgrimages to these holy places."

But much of the time Housman was particularly accurate in terms of topography. One of his disclaimers to verisimilitude included the name of Abdon under Clee; but J.L. Bradbury ('Poetry and Place in A.E. Housman' *HSJ*, 1979 pp.11–19) has shown that although the village is now derelict, in 1895 it would have looked very much as he pictured it in *LP* XLI, 'Fancy's Knell.' He knew Ludlow well, with its tower which really does play 'The conquering hero comes' (*ASL* III). He knew Wenlock Edge and the Wrekin and, of course, Shrewsbury, which furnishes an example not only of his accuracy to place, but his imaginative use of it:

> They hang us now in Shrewsbury jail:
> The whistles blow forlorn,

75

And trains all night groan on the rail
    To men that die at morn.
                            (*ASL* IX)

Shrewsbury prison stands on a hill overlooking the railway station
at the point where the railway crosses the river Severn (in fact the
platforms extend on to the bridge itself). Across the river from the
prison the Wolverhampton line turns east in what is a sweeping
approach to the station, in the arc of which are rows of sidings.
Although it suffered quite a demise in post-Beeching years, it was
once a very busy station, the gateway to north and mid-Wales; but
even today the noise of shunting, or a late night mail-train taking
the curve of the bend, blown across the open land between the
Abbey and the station, is precisely as the poem describes it.

Another poem concerning Shrewsbury is *ASL* XXVIII, 'The
Welsh Marches,' which describes the town "Islanded in Severn
stream". The Severn in fact forms a wide quasi-circular loop
around the hill on which the old centre of the town stands. The
opening of the loop faces north-east, making the town an ideal
defensive outpost against Wales with its castle, across the station
from the prison, plugging the narrow neck of land.

The flag of morn in conqueror's state
Enters at the English gate:
The vanquished eve, as night prevails
Bleeds upon the road to Wales.

This stanza gains in resonance when one realizes not only that there
is a bridge crossing eastwards called the English Bridge, but also
one on the opposite side of the town, called the Welsh Bridge. The
town, as the poem suggests, is the site of ancient battles between the
Welsh and English (Saxons).

So, if Shropshire is a county of the mind, this is not really so in
respect of topography, despite Hughley and the inclusion in *A
Shropshire Lad* of the poem 'Bredon Hill' (*ASL* XXI), which is
actually a hill in his native Worcestershire. Even the inclusion of
Knighton in *ASL* L, with its "When I was a Knighton Lad",
though the town is technically Welsh, does not really change much:
it is right on the border, being built on the river which separates
England from Wales at this point. It is the human face of

Housman's county which bears no relation to the day-to-day reality of the Welsh Marches. His tragic couples, soldiers and love-lorn youths are the stock characters of English pastoral and romantic poetry. Admittedly in '1887' he alludes quite accurately to the exploits of the King's Shropshire Light Infantry, but this is an instance that stands out in contrast to a general atmosphere which has more to do with certain idealised notions about rural life, than with those lives themselves.

Firstly, the matter of language. Housman was no William Barnes, nor even a Thomas Hardy in this respect. Whereas Barnes accurately reproduced the dialect of his native Dorset, and Hardy in his poetry used dialect words as part of a wider linguistic compass, Housman has clearly little knowledge of and no interest in authentic Shropshire dialect. When his characters seem to approach some semblance of folk-speech, it is usually a mixture of archaism and pastiche, as in this from *ASL* LXII, 'Terence, this is stupid stuff':

> Then the world seemed none so bad,
> And I myself a sterling lad;
> And down in lovely muck I've lain,
> Happy till I woke again.
> Then I saw the morning sky:
> Heigho, the tale was all a lie . . . .

Housman's frequent, even compulsive, use of the word "lad", which cannot help but be irritating at times, is nothing to do with realism, for in that case the poems would be sprinkled with "my mon". In all the poems I can only find one example of what might seem to be a genuine Shropshire dialect usage, in *ASL* XXV: "We needs must jangle, till at last/We fought and I was beat". The *Shropshire Word-Book* (1879) has for "jangling", "the idle talking which is fruitful of 'evil speaking, lying, and slandering'", as a common Shropshire word. But to "jangle" as "to dispute, wrangle" is in the *Oxford English Dictionary* as an archaic sense, and it is almost certainly in this respect that he uses the word.

Just as there is little in the poems that corresponds to the language of the rural community, so the society described in them is a series of generalizations, almost the cliches of country life, with none of the particularity to be found in the poems of Hardy and

Barnes, or in more recent poets like Seamus Heaney and R.S. Thomas. Housman himself claimed not to be interested in country folk, and when Percy Withers stopped during a walk to pass a few words with one of the locals, he impatiently walked on. There is a strange paradox enacted in *A Shropshire Lad*. In the first half of the book, which deals mainly with characters in the Shropshire setting itself, life on the land is something to be escaped from, or so it seems. There is drinking and football and love, for which the lovers in 'Bredon Hill' defy the routine church-going that is expected of them. And in a different order of escape there is the army, and death. But the second half of the book, when the central figure of the poems has left for London, presents Shropshire as "the land of lost content" the place of happiness and innocence, which can never be reclaimed; the true pastoral idyll, which it never represented before, being then a place of betrayal, crime and punishment.

Seeing the volume in this light, it is perhaps possible to understand the dangers of trying to see the poems as forming a sequence. The U.S. critic Bobby Joe Leggett has made the most competent attempt at such an interpretation, arguing that the book traces the development of the character of Terence Hearsay, from the trials of innocence in Shropshire, through to the more mature disillusionment of the London poems. I have two major objections to this: first, that the arrangement of the poems within the two halves of the book is not sequential, although they do occasionally fall into groups with similar themes; secondly, the persona of most of the earlier poems is not particularly innocent (though he observes innocence betrayed), nor has he become significantly wiser by the end of the volume. No theory that tries to identify a settled structure in *A Shropshire Lad* really seems to work. What unifies the volume, apart from the pastoral setting in Shropshire, is the difficult figure of Terence Hearsay, at once the fictional author of and principal persona in the poems themselves.

Terence has remained a very elusive figure for Housman critics. Apart from knowing that the volume was to be called 'Poems by Terence Hearsay,' the only other evidence for him is the penultimate poem, *ASL* LXII, ' "Terence, this is stupid stuff" ', a dialogue between Terence and a friend, one of only two poems that mention him by name, as the book stands. From this it appears clear that he is the poet responsible for the preceding verses and that he is, in fact, the 'Shropshire Lad.' Apart from this, we have Housman's own words on the matter, from his letter to Maurice Pollet: "The Shropshire Lad is an imaginary figure, with some-thing of my temper and view of life. Very little in the book is biographical" (*P.&P.* p.469). It is interesting that it has become quite common to see Terence as a simple rustic poet, producing poems that are essentially simple and naive, whose ironies and insights are the product of their other author, A.E. Housman, playing the role of ventriloquist or puppet-master. There are many problems with this approach. It necessarily complicates our reading of the poems, in that you have to separate the poet-persona from the true poet and place the second on a higher plane of perception; meanwhile the poems continuously refuse to let themselves be broken down into two distinct readings, the simple one for the rustic poet, and the more subtle one for Housman and us. Housman's irony tends to be too inherent in the structure of the poems to allow this kind of separation.

> They tolled the one bell only,
>   Groom there was none to see,
> The mourners followed after,
>   And so to church went she,
>   And would not wait for me.
>   (*ASL* XXI, 'Bredon Hill')

I have read an interpretation of this poem, which has the rustic persona of the poem (Terence?) actually accusing his lover of a kind of unfaithfulness here, as if he thought she died to spite him, so 'unsophisticated' was he taken to be. It is not uncommon for literary people to assume country people are lacking in some of their emotional equipment. Leggett is right to oppose this kind of slander by demonstrating the sophisticated nature of Terence's defence of his poetry in ' "Terence, this is stupid stuff" ', in his book *The Poetic Art of A.E. Housman* (Univ. of Nebraska Press, Lincoln, USA, 1978).

It seems much more sensible to me to view Terence as a kind of *alter ego* for Housman, endowed not only with something of his temper and view of life, but with his poetic talent as well. At times he presents himself as a character in a poem, as in *ASL* VIII

'Farewell to barn and stack and tree', where he is the silent receiver of his friend's confession to murder. At times he is totally invisible: *ASL* XLIV, the poem about the Woolwich Cadet, whilst not biographical as such, is a poem we can assume to be very close to Housman's heart, something written without Terence Hearsay in mind. Indeed, a lot of the volume appears to have been written without, or before, the idea of Terence. The first lines of ' "Terence, this is stupid stuff" ' appeared in the notebooks in August 1894, about a month or so before 'Farewell to barn and stack and tree', the only other poem that mentions him by name. Somewhere around a quarter of the poems had been written in the five or so years preceding this. It seems reasonable to assume that the first appearance of his name coincides approximately with Housman's first thinking of the idea of making him the 'poet' of his first volume, especially as that first appearance is in the poem in which he explains the motives behind his poetry.

Just as some of *A Shropshire Lad* predates Terence, so a lot of *Last Poems* consists of poems written in 1894–5 and bearing clear marks of his presence, *LP* XXIII 'In the morning, in the morning', for example; although a later poem like *LP* XX 'The night is freezing fast' (1922) still sounds as if it belongs to the fictional poet, with its familiar use of the Christian name: "And chiefly I remember/How Dick would hate the cold". So the fact is that the majority of the poems in *A Shropshire Lad* were written after Housman had conceived of the idea of a rural *alter ego*. It does not seem likely to me that he did this merely because he originally wanted to publish *Poems by Terence Hearsay* pseudonymously. We do not know whether the original manuscript, offered under that title to Macmillan, referred at any point to its real author. But if Housman had wanted to keep his own authorship secret, he very quickly dropped the idea when Arthur Pollard offered him a better title — he could still have used Terence's name. So whatever his real function in the book, it isn't that. I think we have to imagine something of the freedom the creation of this poet-mask would have given Housman, both in his writing, and in placing what he wrote before the public. This freedom would be complemented by the freedoms he took in his recreation of Shropshire.

Terence Hearsay is a fictional poet in a fictional world. It may be true that this world is first presented to us in a poem about a real event, *ASL* I '1887', describing Queen Victoria's jubilee, but we are soon observing the process of the construction of a kind of microcosm. In this process, the difference between A. E. Housman and his poet, is that what Terence observes from his vantage within this mythic land is actually being created by Housman. This allows us to dispense with any notion of Housman being more intelligent or sophisticated than the Shropshire Lad: they merely exist in different dimensions. Like all created worlds this one needs its myths, and Housman very soon goes about providing them. *ASL* VIII 'Farewell to barn and stack and tree', which has Terence confronted by a man who has killed his brother, is actually a transformation of the story Cain and Abel. The unnamed Cain figure in the poem is, like his original, a "tiller of the ground",' though we don't know if his victim Maurice kept the sheep (incidentally, though it may be unintended, there is certainly some irony in the note to the next poem in the book, which explains: "Hanging in chains was called keeping sheep by moonlight"). It is sometimes presumed by critics that the murderer in the poem is going to take his own life (or knows that the law will do it for him, since the next poem happens to be about a hanged man), but nothing in the poems actually tells us that. What lines like "She had two sons at rising day,/To-night she'll be alone" actually suggest, if one thinks, is the wanderings of Cain, the exile from the homeland. The difference between Housman's version of the myth and that in the Bible, is that his is a secularized rereading of it. The murderer answers to the sympathetic ear of Terence, not to the damning voice of the Lord.

The same is true of another poem based on the Bible, *ASL* XLVII, 'The Carpenter's Son.' On the literal level it is the speech — as with *ASL* VIII it is presented in inverted commas — of a man condemned to be hanged, bemoaning his fate:

> "Oh, at home had I but stayed
> 'Prenticed to my father's trade,
> Had I stuck to plane and adze,
> I had not been lost, my lads.
>
> "Then I might have built perhaps
> Gallows-trees for other chaps,
> Never dangled on my own,
> Had I but left ill alone."

Up to this point any resemblance to Christ's crucifixion seems incidental; while the idea of the Messiah suggesting he would have done better to make gallows for others seems blasphemous. But then Housman makes the parallel undeniable:

> "Here hang I, and right and left
> Two poor fellows hang for theft:
> All the same's the luck we prove,
> Though the midmost hangs for love."

He is dying because he could not leave 'ill' alone, but that 'ill' seems to have been love. What that love is we are not told, but then again, keeping in mind the redemptive value of Christ's death, we have the lines which end both the first and last stanzas: "Fare you well, for ill fare I:/Live, lads, and I will die". Housman's Christ will not rise from the dead; nor does he have anyone to call to from the gallows, asking them why they have forsaken him; for he belongs to a world without a God, a world created by an atheist out of the material of the Christian world in which he lived. The effect of the poem is similar to that of Millais's painting *Christ in the House of his Parents* (1849), where the Biblical figures are presented as all too human and unprepossessing. It is a shock. But Millais is making a different point, for his rather gawky Christchild nonetheless carries the stigmata and is still the divine presence amongst the fallenness of even his own body. Housman goes a stage further; for his Christ is fallen and the only redemption he can give is a purely earthly gesture; in effect "I'm dying, and you're not — live on". Any humanist rereading of the Gospels can say little more than that.

A case could be made with respect to *ASL* XLIII, 'The Immortal Part', that this poem is a reworking in part of Ezekiel, Chapter 37, where the Lord shows the prophet the valley full of bones and asks him, "Son of man, can these bones live?" In Housman's poem it is the bones that speak, demanding the death of the flesh:

> "When shall this slough of sense be cast,
> This dust of thoughts be laid at last,
> The man of flesh and soul be slain
> And the man of bone remain?"

Whereas in the Old Testament story the bones are reclothed in flesh, and life is called back into the dead, Housman takes the progression in reverse: death is not the removal of flesh from the bone, but the fact of having it there in the first place, since death is a continuous process of decay and "The immortal bones obey control/Of dying flesh and dying soul". It is as if the bones in the valley refused to be brought back to life, since they see themselves as the ultimate fruits of human existence:

> "Wanderers eastward, wanderers west,
> Know you why you cannot rest?
> 'Tis that every mother's son
> Travails with a skeleton."

"Travails" is an example of Housman's often-ignored verbal dexterity: not only does it include both meanings of the word — to suffer the pangs of childbirth, and to make a painful and laborious effort — but it also echoes the wandering of the previous lines with its pun on 'travels'. There is no prophet with his God to call these bones to life, and they don't need it. It becomes a myth for a godless land, a religion for the irreligious.

This mythmaking is one aspect of the creation of the Salopian universe. I have concentrated on his reworkings of Biblical material, but there are others, such as *ASL* XX, 'Oh fair enough are sky and plain', which is the story of Narcissus, already referred to in *ASL* XV. But there are other aspects to this world which Housman builds up, other recastings of reality. The military theme is one of these. It is such a strong note in the collection that Kegan Paul originally tried to persuade him to turn the book into a "romance of enlistment". Although the idea may seem absurd to us now, the words 'romance of enlistment' do adequately describe this aspect of *A Shropshire Lad*. Enlistment is both an escape and a duty, it seems; but it is an escape into death, and a duty to die. 'Reveille' (*ASL* IV) catches the note of temptation, the desire for wider horizons:

> Up, lad, up, 'tis late for lying:
>   Hear the drums of morning play;
> Hark, the empty highways crying
>   "Who'll beyond the hills away?"

The notion of life as a lonely march towards death is taken up by poems with non-martial themes, and is perhaps best expressed in *ASL* XXXVI 'White in the moon the long road lies', where the moment of death, however, is deferred in the idea of ceaselessly walking the globe. In 'Reveille' death is merely journey's end, the traveller's rest:

> Clay lies still, but blood's a rover;
>   Breath's a ware that will not keep.
> Up, lad: when the journey's over
>   There'll be time enough to sleep.

It is to clay, of course, the blood returns, a Christian reference to which Housman returns again and again, and which is especially poignant with regard to the soldier, who dies in the mud and dust of the battlefield. In 'The Recruit' (*ASL* III) death is seen more in the context of the battle, the idealised notion of battle as a fight between comrades and the enemy, where the soldier can "make the foes of England/Be sorry you were born". And here the act of dying for and among one's fellows becomes important, that one should "make the hearts of comrades/Be heavy where you die". The one true form of fellowship in the poems is the death-pact of the army, and ideas of friendship and death are never far apart:

> Far and near and low and louder
>   On the roads of earth go by,
> Dear to friends and food for powder,
>   Soldiers marching, all to die.
>   (*ASL* XXXV)

It is a strange obsessive trait that friendship and death are almost always twinned. In *ASL* XXV 'This time of year a twelvemonth past' the quarrel between friends, which appears to lead to the winner getting the girl, is in fact concluded by the arbitrary death of "the better man". *ASL* XXIV 'Say, lad, have you things to do?' is an appeal for friendship to be answered, but again the end is death: "Use me ere they lay me low/Where a man's no use at all". In *ASL* XXXIV, 'The New Mistress', the jilted lover turns to the army, as a soldier of the Queen (his new mistress on one level only). Variations on the phrase "sick am I to see you" occur in each of the four stanzas. In the first, the woman says this to her lover. In the second he says of the uniform that the Queen "will not be sick to see me if I only keep it clean". In the third, it is the sergeant who "may be sick to see me but he treats me very kind". All this playing on the phrase of rejection culminates in the final stanza: "Where the standing line wears thinner and the dropping dead lie thick;/And the enemies of England they shall see me and be sick". It is a succession of mock lovers, ending in the one he will kill or else be killed by.

I could gather examples for a long time, to prove the strength of the connection the poems forge between fellowship and death, and between love and death: because lovers in Housman's poems are, like soldiers, always dying and being replaced by other lovers. And here I would like to present something which is as close to a key to the poems as we are ever likely to get. The notion of dying for one's fellow men, which I mentioned as being important in the previous chapter, is, in fact, the covert route by which A.E. Housman's homosexuality finds expression. This may explain how death is the prime mover in the world of Shropshire; beyond the retelling of myth, beyond the martial theme (which itself occupies only half a dozen poems in *A Shropshire Lad*), beyond the theme of young love, there is death, weaving in and out of all of them. The poet and critic Stephen Spender made the comment long ago that, despite this prevalence, there is so little feeling for the dead, or curiosity about death. But he missed what actually does happen. Death is the alternative sweetheart of the poetry:

> It nods and curtseys and recovers
>   When the wind blows above,
> The nettle on the graves of lovers
>   That hanged themselves for love.
>
> The nettle nods, the wind blows over,
>   The man, he does not move,
> The lover of the grave, the lover
>   That hanged himself for love.
>   (*ASL* XVI)

I quote the whole of this short poem, which is as explicit about the love/death relationship as anything the poet wrote, in the way it turns its meaning around on itself. The lovers (plural) of the first stanza hang themselves for the love of another; the singular lover of the second stanza hangs himself — it is implied by the still ambiguous "lover of the grave" — for the love of death. Yet the real heart of the poem is the seamless way that one meaning of suicide slips into the other, as if they were two sides of the same coin which flips over with the stanza-break. But do we then have to take the conjoining of sex and death (a consummation reinforced by psycho-analysis, one of whose truisms is that death is symbolic of sexual climax) and apply it to the instances when death seems bound up with the experience of male companionship?

I want to turn to *ASL* XXII:

> The street sounds to the solders' tread,
>   And out we troop to see:
> A single redcoat turns his head,
>   He turns and looks at me.

This single, almost incidental moment becomes epiphanic; it is a sudden meeting of two souls whose relationship will be one of total absence, but which, thanks to the luminosity of the memory, and perhaps thanks even to poetry itself, will still be a relationship:

> My man, from sky to sky's so far,
>   We never crossed before;
> Such leagues apart the world's ends are,
>   We're like to meet no more;
>
> What thoughts at heart have you and I
>   We cannot stop to tell;
> But dead or living, drunk or dry,
>   Soldier, I wish you well.

This may remind one of a letter he sent to his stepmother during his first visit to London, a letter full of the young tourist's impressions of the city, its Cathedrals and Museums (he was fifteen at the time): "I think of all I have seen, what has most impressed me is — the Guards. This may be barbarian, but it is true". (*Letters* p. 6) Fascination with soldiers was not something confined to young girls, and the Guards themselves were well known in homosexual circles as a regiment where prostitutes could be found. The poem could almost be describing one of Housman's experiences in

London, but such a biographical link is not necessary: what we are looking at is a hidden code within the poetry, a code which not only associates sex with death, and the desire for death, but which also seems to suggest something subtly different, namely, that (to turn a trope from the Bible) the wages of love is death. In the godless world of *A Shropshire Lad* love is forbidden, and this law will enact the inevitable separation through death. Only in death can lovers stay together, when they cannot know it:

> Lovers lying two and two
>   Ask not whom they sleep beside,
> And the bridegroom all night through
>   Never turns him to the bride.
> (ASL XII)

In *ASL* XI the sex-death nexus is reinforced through a radical ambiguity. The first stanza is the lover's plea for his love to be reciprocated: "Therefore, since I go to-morrow,/Pity me before". Where he goes is, of course, the place from which there is no return:

> In the land to which I travel,
>   The far dwelling, let me say —
> Once, if here the couch is gravel,
>   In a kinder bed I lay,
> And the breast the darnel smothers
>   Rested once upon another's
>   When it was not clay.

In the context of the first stanza it might seem that "another's" breast may be that of the lover. But "another" may be one other than the lover. If "clay" refers to the earth to which the living body returns, then the verse expresses the idea of consolation, of having been loved before one dies. But "clay" may be the living body, the body of flesh and blood, beyond which there is an eternity without life or substance, the eternity from which we came and to which we return, and the only bosom where there is any rest: the lover, death. No earthly love escapes this other love, be it love of woman, or love of comrades: it comes as a punishment. A very public punishment too — either the heroic death at the hands of the enemy, or the public execution. Hanging carries no shame in these poems, is no register of guilt, and the hanged man, as in 'The Carpenter's Son', is usually a better man than those who outlive him:

> There sleeps in Shrewsbury jail to-night,
>   Or wakes, as may betide,
> A better lad, if things went right,
>   Than most that sleep outside.
>   (*ASL* IX)

Occasionally they kill themselves for love, and like the Woolwich Cadet, enact the punishment upon themselves.

The only way I can read this cruel world is to go full circle, to say that the pastoral world created by A.E. Housman is in fact a metaphor for the very world in which he lived, a world where love, a certain form of love, is illegal. And, as in *A Shropshire Lad*, it 'dare not speak its name.' How deliberate the strategy was we can only guess, but what is happening seems quite clear: it is not so much that Housman was trying to write about his homosexuality without actually saying as much; what he does is create a context in which emotions that would normally have to be suppressed (and were perhaps internally repressed) can find an outlet. He could not describe Victorian society as he experienced it directly, so he reproduced it on the level of fantasy, at the same time reproducing himself within this fantasy in the figure of Terence Hearsay. What emerges is a kind of sick pastoral, shorn of ideals, idylls and any guiding principles but the arbitrary "laws of God, the laws of man".

I want to stress, however, that I would not read everything in the poems this way, for there are clearly other elements present which deserve to be given their own space. But the underlying tenor of Housman's work, which has been labelled morbidity, adolescence and pessimism, is due almost entirely to this cloaking procedure. English pastoral poetry, from Sidney and Spenser onwards, has had strong links with allegory, where characters in the poetry symbolize certain moral or spiritual qualities, or elements in society, sometimes even embodied in disguised portraits of real people. I do not think that any such resemblances could be traced in *A Shropshire Lad*; in fact, I think it would be unwise to try and find them — the effect of these poems, many of which were inserted in the volume *post hoc*, is more fragmentary than that — but they do work on an impressionistic level for which the word allegory may be a useful descriptive term. Furthermore two of Housman's poems, 'The Merry Guide' (*ASL* XLII) and 'Hell Gate' (*LP* XXXI), do appear to be distinctly allegorical narratives. In the first of these, the speaker of the poem is approached by "a youth that trod,/With feathered cap on forehead, /And poised a golden rod". This Merry Guide leads him across the countryside, refusing to say where they are going, refusing in fact to say anything. The journey is endless, as "We two fare on for ever,/But not we two alone":

> With the great gale we journey
>   That breathes from gardens thinned,
> Borne in the drift of blossoms
>   Whose petals throng the wind;
>
> Buoyed on the heaven-heard whisper
>   Of dancing leaflets whirled
> From all the woods that autumn
>   Bereaves in all the world.

These are "the fluttering legion/Of all that ever died", and the merry guide is Hermes, as confirmed by the final lines describing his "feet that fly on feathers,/And serpent-circled wand", here performing his role of leading the dead to the underworld. Except that here there is a difference. Is the speaker in the poem dead, or has he been lured into this limbo? Because the journey is described as being endless; there is no underworld they go to, so the smiling, enticing guide is leading them nowhere. Hermes is also the God of lying; but here he never utters a word, and all he deceives them with is his smile. It may be that they are content to follow it. The enticement which the guide represents clearly has some sexual edge, and at one point the poem (which is the earliest in the volume) presages *ASL* XXII, about the fleeting glance between the speaker and a soldier:

> With mien to match the morning
>   And gay delightful guise
> And friendly brows and laughter
>   He looked me in the eyes.

It is another silent look, but this time the smile — and there is almost only the smile — is always before him. The idea of *ASL* XXII, which is that the glance, though fleeting, remains as a luminous memory, is re-enacted here, but the luminous memory, the epiphanic moment, has become a trap and a lure. I put it this way round, even though 'The Merry Guide' was written first, because it is almost as if the earlier poem were an allegorical treatment of the experience presented in the later one; a treatment delving more into the psychological consequences of that experience. It is 'almost' this, but may also be one way Housman found of dealing with his relationship with Moses Jackson.

The other allegorical poem in A.E. Housman's work is the one from *Last Poems* (XXXI) which he admitted to being most unsure of, partly no doubt because at 104 lines it is by far the longest of his mature poems. The speaker is led to the gates of Hell by a "dark conductor", a satanic version of the Merry Guide, a "sombre guide", in fact. He meets Sin and Death on the drawbridge, at which moment the sentry, who has been pacing back and forth in his "finery of fire", turns, "Looked, and knew me, and was Ned". This sentry, seeing his old friend is also damned, mutinies, shooting the guide, who is of course Satan. This murder, an instinctive act of comradeship and love against all the odds, causes the absolute ruin of Hell. In the end there are just the two of them:

> Tyranny and terror flown
> Left a pair of friends alone,
> And beneath the nether sky
> All that stirred was he and I.

The fire about Ned dies, leaving them both just human. The last lines echo the story of Sodom and Gomorrah, except that in this backward glance nobody is turned to salt:

> Midmost of the homeward track
> Once we listened and looked back;
> But the city, dusk and mute,
> Slept, and there was no pursuit.

Against all the despair and pessimism of his poetry (and there is more in Housman than in all of Hardy's vast output, though both denied being pessimists) he pitches this piece of gloomy, melodramatic wish fulfilment. As so often, I find myself answering poem with poem. *AP* II is a poem generally accepted to be about Moses Jackson; it begins:

> Oh were he and I together,
>   Shipmates on the fleeted main,
> Sailing through the summer weather
>   To the spoil of France or Spain.

The tone is adolescent, perhaps deliberately so, drawing in the kinds of emotions and daydreams a youth may have about his best friend. It is a tone which shadows many of his poems about comradeship; at times it seems as if war is a game of soldiers with fatal results. It has led to a lot of criticism and one interesting defence, from Stephen Spender, who claims that "for a poet of limited aims, strong ideals, and a perfectionist technique" it may be "an admirable theme" (Stephen Spender, *The Making of a Poem*, Hamish Hamilton, London, 1955, p.162). He goes on to say:

> This theme is the stage of life where idealistic and sensuous impulses establish a precarious truce. The body is so beautiful that the spirit can almost accept it as pure aesthetic delight. Indeed, an ambiguous phase, when the metamorphosis of the ideas of the mind into realizations of the body seems one continual process of idealistic love. Then the pure are truly pure, and to them all things remain pure, and there is no loss of innocence in any love.

Whilst this may not correspond to our own ideas about adolescence, it seems to capture a certain element of importance to Housman; the idealism of 'Say, lad, have you things to do?' (*ASL* XXIV) and others about male friendship. It can be both a strength and weakness in the poems. *AP* II, quoted above, is one of his more childish attempts, failing to achieve any real emotional depth, but elsewhere it is capable of producing some of his best verse, as in 'If truth in hearts that perish'(*ASL* XXXIII). But Spender seems to imply that adolescence *is* Housman's theme, and I would really like to emphasise that it is more a tone that he makes use of, one that actually cloaks the theme which really concerns him, asexualising it.

We have now moved to poems outside of *A Shropshire Lad*, but it should be fairly clear by now that little in Housman's work changed with time. *Last Poems* still contains Shropshire poems which would lie well alongside the ostensible utterances of Terence Hearsay. The function which Shropshire served was one it continued to serve, and Terence Hearsay merely became subsumed into Housman's own writing persona, or mask. So it is a frequent occurrence to find critics talking about Housman's rustic persona in the context of poems in the later book. One consequence of internalising this *alter ego*, and no longer needing to focus upon him so much as a vehicle for the poems, is a greater emotional range in the second book, with poems like 'Astronomy' (*LP* XVII) and 'Revolution' (*LP* XXXVI). These not only make use of the professor's interest in the heavens, but provide a rare note which dwarfs human concerns against the vastness of the universe.

There is one more thing to say about Shropshire. It is probably obvious now that the county of the mind I have been describing is not really compatible with the "land of lost content" looked back to in the London poems of *A Shropshire Lad*. It is interesting that these London poems describe little of the city itself: what they do seem to do is present us with a different vision of the county. It is as if, when Terence Hearsay travels "through the wild green hills, of Wyre" on the now disused railway line between Ludlow and Kidderminster (Staffs) the county is changing behind him. He relives the old truism that home is always more dear to you when you're away from it. But he also introduces something quite different. If Shropshire as a backdrop for certain emotions and the relationships which produce them is one thing, then Shropshire as a memory, a place below the horizon, is something else. It is no longer a county of the mind, but an image in the mind. This is the sunset land of green hills which the young Alfred would gaze at from 'Mount Pisgah' near Fockbury House, probably imbuing it with notions of contentment from childhood memories, feeling that with his mother's death his own childhood was now over. Many of his emotional needs may have been projected into that landscape, always to be associated with it. This may be an unforgivable piece of biographical projection, but it describes the effect which this other version of Shropshire has in the poems of the second half of *A Shropshire Lad*. This is the condition of being Moses (as opposed to Moses Jackson); you know you will never reach the promised land, and you would never find it how you feel it, if you did.

There is something Moses-like about the position taken by the speaker of *ASL* XXXI 'On Wenlock Edge the wood's in trouble'. The panoramic view of the first stanza takes in Wenlock Edge, the Wrekin and the Severn that flows between them:

> On Wenlock Edge the wood's in trouble;
>   His forest fleece the Wrekin heaves;
> The gale, it plies the saplings double,
>   And thick on Severn snow the leaves.

There is no Canaan here, but a countryside "in trouble": what this trouble signifies, except the natural action of the wind, is not yet clear. "Snow" suggests winter, but this seems to go no further. The first lines of the next stanza give us a clue: " 'Twould blow like this through holt and hanger/When Uricon the city stood". Uricon is Viroconium, the Roman city at Wroxeter, about four miles southeast of Shrewsbury. We are back two thousand years, but with the same "old wind in the old anger":

> Then, 'twas before my time, the Roman
>   At yonder heaving hill would stare:
> The blood that warms an English yeoman,
>   The thoughts that hurt him, they were there.

In some ways this is a counter statement to 'The Welsh Marches' (*ASL* XXVIII) where "The Saxon got me on the slave" setting up a racial struggle in the blood as Saxon and Welsh identities fight in "The knot that makes one flesh of two". The Roman, separated from the speaker of *ASL* XXXI by vast tracts of history, is on the contrary almost the mirror-image of him. Now the wind is "the gale of life", seen not as a positive breath, but as a more troublesome force that blows "through woods in riot", so "The tree of man was never quiet". It is a power that agitates, that threatens to overwhelm us.

The gale, it plies the saplings double,
  It blows so hard, 'twill soon be gone:
To-day the Roman and his trouble
  Are ashes under Uricon.

In this final stanza, life and the gale will soon be over. The "trouble" of the Roman recalls "the woods in trouble" of the poem's first line. It is the same for Roman and yeoman, as much a part of them as life itself. The poem sees the individual as a mere event in the passage of "the old wind in the old anger", which makes compatriots of people separated by millennia. But the poem works because, unlike my commentary, this deeper meaning emerges gradually. Initially we are presented with a real wind in a real landscape; for a moment Shropshire seems more than Housman's fiction. The invocation of history works in a similar way as the reference to real events in '1887' (*ASL* I); it introduces a kind of hard evidence which counters the entirely imaginery nature of "the Roman". Only the archaic word 'yeoman' suggests the pastoral setting of the volume as a whole, and I am inclined to see it as weakening the poem, however slightly.

But the poem is larger than this quibble. The poet and the Roman look out across the same land, although another wood was there before and the city of Uricon is no more. It is not a vision of the Promised Land, but of life and one's own small part in it. A part that has always been played before.

A Lyric Style

When writing about Housman's poetry, it is usual to spend an inordinate amount of time discussing the influences upon his style. It is something I want to avoid, so I'll begin by doing it. He acknowledged three major influences; Shakespeare's songs, the Scottish Border ballads and the German poet Heine. He didn't feel the need to acknowledge the Bible as such, but he was steeped in it. In the back of Grant Richards's *Housman 1897–1936* is an appendix by G.B.A. Fletcher listing, among other things, "undoubted and probable reminiscences". Two of the twelve references to the Bible here come from the short book of Ecclesiastes, not many, but anomalous in relation to the book's size and importance within the Bible as a whole. But its influence on Housman goes further. In a letter to Laurence, written soon after the publication of *A Shropshire Lad*, he writes:

> Kate [his sister] writes to say that she likes the verse better than the sentiments. The sentiments, she then goes on to say, appear to be taken from the book of Ecclesiastes. To prefer my versification to the sentiments of the Holy Ghost is decidedly flattering, but it strikes me as a trifle impious.
>
> (*P.&P.* p.451)

Not that Ecclesiastes could really be said to express the sentiments of the Holy Ghost. The figure of the Preacher is troubled by the hardships and apparent pointlessness of life, finding little consolation but a wisdom that prepares for the worst:

> Then I looked on all the works that my hands had wrought, and on the labour that I had laboured to do: and, behold, all was vanity and vexation of spirit, and there was no profit under the sun.
>
> (Ecc. ii 11)

Because the good and the sinful in the end get the same reward, it pays to obey God's laws without trying to be excessively virtuous. In other moods, however, he accepts the benefits of earthly pleasures: "Go thy way, eat thy bread with joy, and drink thy wine with a merry heart; for now God accepteth thy works" (Ecc. ix 7). Or as it appears slightly earlier:

> Then I commended mirth, because a man hath no better thing under the sun, than to eat, and to drink, and to be merry: for that shall abide with him of his labour the day of his life, which God giveth him under the sun.
>
> (Ecc. viii 15)

It is a note which Housman strikes in *LP* IX, 'The chestnut casts his flambeaux, and the flowers . . .', with its drinking theme and its defiant view of the universe and "Whatever brute and blackguard made the world". Nowhere is the note more true than in the ending:

> The troubles of our proud and angry dust
>   Are from eternity, and shall not fail.
> Bear them we can, and if we can we must.
>   Shoulder the sky, my lad, and drink your ale.

That last line has been accused of bathos, but I think that is a deliberate ploy, which Housman uses elsewhere to add a touch of irony. In this case, if it isn't an allusion to Ecclesiastes as such, it does gain some strength from that context, where God is no giver of comfort, or even guidance, but a force that lays obstacles and traps for our vanity.

It is no surprise that the two reminiscences of Ecclesiastes found by Fletcher concern death. The first is from Ecc. xi 8: "If a man live many years, and rejoice in them all; yet let him remember the days of darkness, for they shall by many", which Housman turns into:

> If the heats of hate and lust
>   In the house of flesh are strong,
> Let me mind the house of dust
>   Where my sojourn shall be long.
>   (*ASL* XII)

The other is from Ecc. ix 10: "For there is no work, nor device, nor

knowledge, nor wisdom, in the grave". This is transformed in *LP*
V, in the context of the wage paid to a common soldier:

> And I shall have to bate my price,
>   For in the grave, they say,
> Is neither knowledge nor device
>   Nor thirteen pence a day.

These are such straight lifts from the Old Testament book that they
stand out among the list of mainly verbal echoes to the scriptures.
Ecclesiastes, in which the Lord makes no direct intercession but is
an absent figure who has laid down the hard conditions of life and
death, is surely the part of the Bible most amenable to an atheistic
interpretation. As we have seen, the other major use to which
Housman put the Bible was in his secularizing of particular
episodes, creating a kind of *ad hoc* mythology for *A Shropshire Lad*.
In this sense it is not contradictory for an atheist to be so influenced
by a religious text. Housman was brought up in the Church of
England, which he considered the best of all religions, and his loss
of faith must be considered a reaction to the illness and death of his
mother. Christianity had always been a strong feature of his family
life and rejection of it is something that could not have been done
without a struggle. In a sense that struggle was to continue all his
life, and snarls against "Whatever brute and blackguard made the
world", his retellings of Bible stories, and his occasional excursions
into blasphemy, are the ways that it expresses itself in the poetry.
Housman always denied being a 'classical' poet, and it seems odd
that a man so learned in the classics should have produced so little
poetry on such themes, a practice still seen as a kind of donnish
disease. Perhaps being so conversant with the excellencies of Greek
and Roman literature made him wary of trying to imitate. But I
think also that the very strength of his Christianity — stronger in
his rejection of it than many people's is in faith — that plays a great
part in this. Christianity provided him with the myths and the
morality which formed the foundations of his world, of 'Shropshire' in the poetry. They remained, even though the house was in
ruins.

The other influence which touched Housman's work at the core
of its emotional configuration is Heine. Like him Heine has been
charged with self-pity and adolescence: the themes of death and

unrequited love are common to both, often in the form of the two-stanza, first person lyric. They tend to use a simple, almost plain syntax and vocabulary, and their straightforward, ballad-like verse-forms have attracted the attentions of numerous composers. When he wrote the first two stanzas of 'Sinner's Rue' (*LP* XXX) Housman was in fact producing a version (almost a straight translation, except that the order of the stanzas has been reversed) of Heine's 'Am Kreuzweg wird begraben':

> He's buried at the crossroad,
> He who his own hand slew;
> A blue flower springs from earth there,
> The flower of sinner's rue.
>
> I stand at the crossroads sighing;
> The still night chills me through.
> In the moonlight gently trembles
> The flower of sinner's rue.
>
> > (trans. Hal Draper, *The Complete Poems of Heinrich Heine*, Oxford University Press, 1982, p.73)

Here, for comparison's sake, is Housman's version:

> I walked alone and thinking,
> And faint the nightwind blew
> And stirred on mounds at crossways
> The flower of sinner's rue.
>
> Where the roads part they bury
> Him that his own hand slays,
> And so the weed of sorrow
> Springs at the four cross ways.

It appears that the version has influenced the translation in this case. Heine's 'Die Armesündernblum' is "the poor sinner's flower", so it is more than coincidence, surely, that Housman and Draper translate it the same way. But what is really interesting is that far from just producing a version of Heine's poem, the English poet goes on to engage in a form of collaboration with him, adding three of his own stanzas to the two already rendered. He picks the flower which "seemed a herb of healing" and wears it, ending the poem with a stanza which is characteristic of himself, and not of Heine:

Dead clay that did me kindness,
I can do none to you,
But only wear for breastknot
The flower of sinner's rue.

Ending this way, virtually dedicating the poem to fictional suicide, he repeats a movement found in 'Shot? so quick, so clean an ending?' (*ASL* XLIV) and also 'To an Athlete Dying Young' (*ASL* XIX), where "The garland briefer than a girl's", could implicitly refer on one level to the poem that perpetuates the fame death caught at its zenith. Despite Stephen Spender's accusation that he had little feeling for the dead, he frequently wrote poems for dead men, both real and imaginery. In these poems the sense that the lines are being offered up to their subject is almost always present in some form or another. Certainly there is feeling for the dead; but not a feeling of loss, or one of pity, but a kind of fellow feeling, that the writer too stands on the verge of this eternity, from which we all came forth in the first place, and that what is being commemorated — sometimes even humanely celebrated — is the passage from human being to human memory.

A related point concerning Housman and Heine is the relative directions their poems on death take. Note the way that the English poet changes the order of Heine's stanzas, so that a poem which begins with the suicide buried at the crossroad and ends with the 'chill' of the speaker is reversed. The movement is characteristic of A.E.H.'s poems, the movement being from the internal to the external, the personal to the general, the individual to the universal, and makes the tone of his poems less self-pitying, less self-obsessed than Heine's tends to be. This is only a generalisation, and is not true in every case; but it has particular relevance to those poems where he commemorates death.

The influence of the Scottish Border ballads is more a matter of general thematic and stylistic similarities than of any direct borrowings on Housman's behalf. The simple four-line stanza, and the avoidance in much of the poetry of Latin-derived words in favour of those with Anglo-Saxon roots, are too common to need specific examples here. But occasional poems go beyond this, their themes and structure producing what are essentially pastiche ballads. 'The True Lover' (*ASL* LIII) is an almost notorious case in point. A man visits the woman he is in love with. It is what is poetically called the dead of night, "When lovers crown their vows". She comes to realise that he is a ghost, come to ask for one night of the love which she denied him while he lived, and for which, one presumes, he died. The dead lover, the midnight scene, a ghost, the dialogue form through which she discovers the truth, and a side-order of blood. All these are ingredients of classic ballads, like 'The Wife at Usher's Well', 'Lord Randal' and 'Bonny Barbara Allan.' The trouble is that in the voice of a late-nineteenth century poet these things can come out sounding, not chilling, but ridiculous:

> 'Oh lad, what is it, lad, that drips
>   Wet from your neck on mine?
> What is it falling on my lips,
>   My lad, that tastes of brine?'

> 'Oh like enough 'tis blood, my dear,
>   For when the knife has slit
> The throat across from ear to ear
>   'Twill bleed because of it.'

Obviously the ghost is being a little sarcastic here: it is like the magnificently corny humour that provides relief in the classic horror movies of Karloff and Lugosi (and more recently Vincent Price), but the ballad — not traditionally a vehicle for such irony — is finally flattened by it. The previous build-up, as she slowly discovers that something is wrong, has been too slow and pre-dictable to build up sufficient tension for which this can provide the release-valve. The poem take itself too seriously as a tale. It has been called tasteless, but that is not really the point. Its failure, as Cleanth Brooks has said of Housman's failures and successes generally, is due to a matter of tone. The ironic tone will not fit the ballad, but as we shall see, the ironic circumstance will.

'Is my team ploughing' (*ASL* XXVII) is another ballad-like dialogue. It is a question-and-answer poem between a dead man and his friend, with the former enquiring whether life goes on the same without him. The friend is able to tell him that, yes, his horses still plough, the men still play football and his girl is indeed happy:

> Ay, she lies down lightly,
>   She lies not down to weep:
> Your girl is well contented.
>   Be still, my lad, and sleep.

—a double-edged comfort, since it says nothing of her mourning his death. Having set up this balanced, ambiguous situation, Housman springs the trap in the final stanza, where the friend is asked how it fares with him. The question in context is itself highly ambiguous (though we expect that the dead man doesn't see it this way), saying, "And has he found to sleep in/A better bed than mine?" Unlike 'The True Lover' case, the reply is a masterpiece in the control of ironic tone:

> Yes, lad, I lie easy,
>   I lie as lads would choose;
> I cheer a dead man's sweetheart,
>   Never ask me whose.

The "better bed" than the earth the dead man sleeps in now turns out to be the bed he slept in before: his bed, to speak colloquially. The strength of the last line is its helplessness. It is not so much "Don't ask me because it's better you shouldn't know", as a more pleading, "Please don't force me to admit this". It is one of those phrases which reveal precisely the secret they pretend to conceal.

When Vaughan Williams set this poem to music for his song cycle 'On Wenlock Edge' he purposely left out the two stanzas about football. Housman, who once showed signs of almost physical pain when Percy Withers misguidedly played a record of the cycle to please him, wondered how Vaughan Williams would have liked him cutting a couple of bars from his music. Vaughan Williams's attitude was that anyone who wrote lines like "The goal stands up, the keeper/Stands up to keep the goal" should be grateful to have them excised. I can see his point (and Housman's): the eight lines are legitimate scene-setting, in terms of their subject, but the tone is gauche, neither good poetic language nor anything approaching what one would imagine the character actually saying. They feel too much like an imitation of a ballad. When Housman fails in these poems it is almost always where he is putting words into a character's mouth that are inappropriate to his social and

linguistic situation. As I have said, Housman had no real understanding of rural speech or rural people, and one of the many
elements of the ballad tradition is just such an understanding.

It is perhaps a good time to mention another influence on
Housman which he did not admit to and which, though not as
important in itself, does show something of his interaction with the
popular culture of his time. These influences are the street ballads
and music hall songs of late Victorian and Edwardian England.
Many of the street ballads concern enlistment, and one of his most
successful poems on the theme, 'The New Mistress', could with its
uncharacteristically garrulous line be a rather sophisticated street-
ballad itself:

> 'Oh, sick I am to see you, will you never let me be?
> You may be good for something but you are not good for me.
> Oh, go where you are wanted, for you are not wanted here.
> And that was all the farewell when I parted from my dear.
>
> (*ASL* XXXIV)

The link between Housman and the street ballads may not be
direct, but may filter through Kipling's *Barrack-room Ballads*, a
copy of which Housman sent his brother Herbert as a birthday
present in 1892, and which he obviously admired. As for the music
hall, at least after the turn of the century, Housman's favourite
after-dinner diversion when eating out at one of the big London
restaurants seems to have been a visit to one of these now legendary
places of entertainment. He did not belong to a London gentle-
men's club, and seems to have enjoyed these light-hearted shows
rather more than the serious theatre. Any trace of a direct effect the
music hall might have had on any of his poetry awaits further
research. But there is something which both the street ballads and
the music hall point to, which is of importance in any reading of his
poetry: the role of melodrama.

It is generally and rather loosely assumed that melodrama and
serious literature do not mix. Certainly any poet who employs it is
either a 'popular poet' or no poet at all. But you will find it in poems
by Wordsworth, Hardy and Yeats and in novels by Hardy and
Dickens — all men, called serious thinkers, and a world apart from
what is today assumed (wrongly, I believe) to be the female
preserve of Mills & Boon and TV soap opera. We now live in a

society that produces and consumes melodrama in quantities un-imaginable even fifty years ago; and yet in many ways it is a legacy from the Victorian era. I have neither space nor knowledge to let me theorize about what is good and bad melodrama, only to show that Housman made use of it, deliberately, to both good and ill effect. We have already looked at one of his failures in this respect, 'The True Lover' (*ASL* LIII), which I said takes itself too seriously. The idea of the love-lorn young man taking his life and then returning as a very solid and bloody ghost is certainly melodramatic. What I think the poem tries to do and fails, is to use that melodrama to set up a deeper, more ironical, emotional resonance. But when the ghost comes out with his sarcastic lines about the knife slitting the throat across from "ear to ear" we are not so much made aware of the tragedy of his suicide as of the ridiculousness of the situation itself. 'Bredon Hill' (*ASL* XXI) is another poem whose situation is inherently melodramatic. The way the lovers dismiss the summons of the church bells, the speaker of the poem saying "Oh, peal upon our wedding,/And we will hear the chime,/And come to church in time", makes it predictable that one of them is going to die, or that some other tragedy will come between them and marriage. But the poem, whilst fulfilling what could be called this melodramatic irony (that when they do go to church it will be in very different circumstances to those they expected) gives us something more. First, there is the way the woman's dying is expressed — "My love rose up so early/ And stole out unbeknown/And went to church alone", ironically using the language of betrayal. Then, when the bells return at the end of the poem, there is the speaker's final reaction to them, one of capitulation, yet at the same time deeply ambiguous:

> The bells they sound on Bredon,
>   And still the steeples hum.
> 'Come all to church, good people,'—
>   Oh, noisy bells, be dumb;
>   I hear you, I will come.

It seems fairly clear to me that the speaker intends to obey the summons of the bells in the same way that his lover did. On another level it says something about the atheist Housman's attitude to organised religion: that no matter how much you avoid it in life, it always gets you in the end. The poem discusses two deaths, but there is only one line — "The mourners followed after" — which unequivocally refers to death, while everything else must be inferred from the context. That context is a melodrama.

I hope this shows how Housman could take melodrama as the basis for a poem and produce something which transcends it. It is a skill he shared with Hardy, and I would like to say more about the relationship between the work of these two men who published their first collections of verse within two years of one another, Housman with *A Shropshire Lad* in 1896, and the older Hardy with *Wessex Poems* in 1898. I have already mentioned one important difference between them: Hardy was a rural poet of place, using dialect, local history and an intimate knowledge of topography to build up a simulacrum of a real world; Housman on the other hand had little regard for place, nor for the details of rural life, except as setting and background for his poems. Hardy's Wessex is real; A.E.H.'s Shropshire is really a metaphor. In his treatment of place Hardy is in many ways the heir of William Barnes, who kept a school next door to the architect's office Hardy worked in during his late teens and early twenties. Both are famous as autodidacts, that peculiarly nineteenth century phenomenon, and their inquiring minds were apt to range over diverse areas of the field of knowledge, purely for knowledge's sake. This could amount to a more complete education than the traditional classical training which Housman received. Although the latter was a keen watcher of the changes of the seasons, he does not seem to have had a great deal of knowledge about flora, for instance, and the two disciplines which he did gain a great proficiency in, astronomy and astrology, were subjects relevant to his work on Manilius, although astronomy was a childhood interest. So although to people around him it was hard to reconcile the professor with the Shropshire lad, the fact is that in many ways Housman's work is donnish, in that it influences and ingredients are, in the main, literary. Only people with little or no experience of the countryside could be fooled into thinking Housman a rural poet. What did fool people was his temperament, considered by those with little experience of artists to be unpoetic. That Frank Harris had a similar glimpse of the poet has more to do with a meeting between bohemianism and English conservatism; with more typical literary characters like Bridges,

Blunt and Hardy, Housman got on quite well. They complained that they could not get him to talk, but that was true of most people: other avenues of communication remained open. The figure of the poet-academic is a frequent one in English literary history, Thomas Gray and Christopher Smart being two famous examples. With the expansion of English as a university subject in the last century it is becoming an ever more frequent occurrence. Present-day Oxford University for example has probably half-a-dozen published poets in its teaching staff, most of them in the faculty of English.

Both Hardy and Housman were atheists, but for very different reasons. Hardy, who always remained, in his own words, "churchy", probably lost his faith to nineteenth century rationalism. In early adulthood he read Darwin, Mill and Huxley, to name a few, and developed philosophical objections to Christianity. Along with George Eliot he was one of the first writers to confront the issues raised by the work of Charles Darwin, and out of this interaction came a body of writing shorn of any notion of providence or divine intervention. It was rooted in a kind of fatalism, destiny seeming figured in the impersonal and blind machine-like processes of the evolutionary process. Housman's atheism, as I have shown, was on the contrary a direct response to personal tragedy: his faith simply could not survive the early death of his mother. Whether or not the shift from deism to atheism (which he claimed took place between the ages of thirteen and twenty-one) was in any way aided by his reading is hard to say, but it is unlikely. He had no real interest in philosophy, as his Oxford Greats failure showed, and I doubt that he had any more than a layman's notion of Darwin's ideas.

But although they got there by different routes, there is a great similarity of outlook in their writings when it comes to destiny or fate, and to the role of nature in human affairs. Both envision an impersonal universe, unresponsive to the needs of its individual inhabitants; both, when they refer to the idea of a God, do so in an offended or angry tone, Hardy by replacing 'Him' with 'It', Housman with such lines as "What ever brute and blackguard made the world." In his 'Apology' to *Late Lyrics and Earlier* Hardy denied the charge of pessimism, firstly quoting a line from his own 'In Tenebris':

> If way to the Better there be, it exacts a full look at the Worst:
> that is to say, by the exploration or reality, and its frank
> recognition stage by stage along the survey, with an eye to the best
> consummation possible: briefly, evolutionary meliorism. But it is
> called pessimism nevertheless; under which word, expressed with
> condemnatory emphasis, it is regarded by many as some per-
> nicious new thing (though so old as to underlie the Gospel
> scheme, and even to permeate the Greek drama); and the subject
> is charitably left to decent silence, as if further comment were
> needless.

Housman had similar problems and made his own attempts to
distance himself from the charge of pessimism. I have already
quoted from the letter to Houston Martin where he calls pessimism
'silly' and himself a pejorist as opposed to a meliorist. And in his
poetry he sounds a note very similar — strikingly so — to the line
from his own work which Hardy quotes:

> Therefore, since the world has still
> Much good, but much less good than ill,
> And while the sun and moon endure
> Luck's a chance, but trouble's sure,
> I'd face it as a wise man would,
> And train for ill and not for good.
> (*ASL* LXII)

If the word pessimist had not been universally a criticism, it is
possible that both these writers would have embraced it, but they
did not want to be thought of as people who could only see the dark
side of things, even if their practice in art made it at least a tenable
accusation. They both wanted to make it clear that they had arrived
at their positions after due consideration of the evidence; as
Housman pointed out in the letter to Houston Martin, his pejorism
was arrived at "owing to my observation of the world, not to
personal circumstances" (*P.&P.* p.469). Neither of them seems to
have been willing to acknowledge that "personal circumstances"
might crucially colour one's observations. To that extent they were
both good rationalists, although Housman was sceptical about the
influence of scientific rationalism on society as a whole, as shown by
his disparaging comments on Herbert Spencer in the Introductory
Lecture of 1892. He claimed there that Spencer's idea that

education should, for practical purposes, consist mainly in the sciences, rather overestimated the relevance of science to the life of the average individual.

Among these coincidences of outlook, perhaps the major distinguishing feature stems from Hardy's absorption of the implications of evolutionism. In his poetry, death is an event in a chain of generation, as in 'Old Furniture':

> I see the hands of generations
>   That owned each shiny familiar thing
> In play on its knobs and indentations,
>   And with its ancient fashioning
>   Still dallying:
>
> Hands behind hands, growing paler and paler,
>   As in a mirror a candle-flame
> Shows images of itself, each frailer
>   As it recedes, though the eye may frame
>   Its shape the same.

In this chain of events inheritance is a form of determinism. The short poem 'Heredity' is a clear statement of this Hardyesque determinism. I quote it in full:

> I am the family face;
> Flesh perishes, I live on,
> Projecting trait and trace
> Through time to times anon,
> And leaping from place to place
> Over oblivion.
>
> The years-heired feature that can
> In curve and voice and eye
> Despise the human span
> Of durance — that is I;
> The eternal thing in man,
> That heeds no call to die.

This sense that we carry what is fixed and immutable within us, a kind of claustrophobic world-view, is quite a contrast to Housman's 'Earth and high heaven are fixt of old and founded strong' (*ASL* XLVIII), which pits the personal four-square against the universal, in a way that makes the latter a huge forbidding building, almost a church, from which we cannot escape. Our destinies are written in the stars, and although Housman probably did not believe in astrology as a means of foretelling the future, he refers to it in a number of poems, for example 'Star may plot in heaven with planet' (*LP* XXIX) and 'The stars have not dealt me the worst they could do' (*AP* XVII), and from *MP* XXXIV:

> And if so long I carry
>   The lot that season marred,
> 'Tis that the sons of Adam
>   Are not so evil-starred
>   As they are hard.

Such direct references to astrology are far less important than the way in which Housman uses more astronomical images of the stars as a means of expressing the vastness and immutability of the universe. There are two important poems from *Last Poems* that I would like to quote in full in this context, both because they give graphic illustration of the role astronomy played for Housman, and because they happen to be two of his most impressive pieces.

The first of these poems is the one written on the death of his brother Herbert, 'Astronomy' (*LP* XVII):

> The Wain upon the northern steep
>   Descends and lifts away.
> Oh I will sit me down and weep
>   For bones in Africa.
>
> For pay and medals, name and rank,
>   Things that he has not found,
> He hove the Cross to heaven and sank
>   The pole-star underground.
>
> And now he does not even see
>   Signs of the nadir roll
> At night over the ground where he
>   Is buried with the pole.

The sheer scale of this poem is something not normally associated with the poet of *A Shropshire Lad*; and if there is one sense in which Housman really did develop during the years between the two volumes, this is it. The lines turn on a profound irony: "He hove the Cross to heaven" presents the image of the young soldier performing a Herculean feat, as if he controlled the stars, and not them him. It is quite typical of the poet to describe the coverage of great distance by the change in the night sky above; here it is the loss of the pole-star beneath the horizon, replaced by the Southern Cross. The Pole-star is, of course, the guiding light, the star to steer by in one's life, and Herbert Housman sinks it, loses it. In its place he "heaves the Cross", becomes the Christ-figure, bearing the instrument of sacrifice. And of course, at the end of the poem he suffers the fate seen in the night sky; the star gone, he too is buried. In an almost perfect metaphorical development, Housman brings about the conjunction of Christian symbolism and astrology with astronomical accuracy, in a poem of very real emotional power.

The second of these two near-perfect lyrics is 'Revolution' (*LP* XXXVI), a poem of even greater metaphorical daring:

> West and away the wheels of darkness roll,
>   Day's beamy banner up the east is borne,
> Spectres and fears, the nightmare and her foal,
>   Drown in the golden deluge of the morn.
>
> But over sea and continent from sight
>   Safe to the Indies has the earth conveyed
> The vast and moon-eclipsing cone of night,
>   Her towering foolscap of eternal shade.
>
> See, in mid heaven the sun is mounted; hark,
>   The belfries tingle to the noonday chime.
> 'Tis silent, and the subterranean dark
>   Has crossed the nadir, and begins to climb.

One important thing about this poem is how little it is saying on the purely literal level. Day dawns, and after a while here comes night again. Nobody has died and lies buried, nobody has been unhappy in love, not even Housman; all there has been is a day; but — if this does not sound unwisely tautological — a day on a cosmic scale. The earth moves like the wheels of a gigantic clock, in a motion so sure and imperturbable that even the rather gothic scene-setting of "Spectres and fears, the nightmare and her foal" has become something more real and threatening when we finally come to "the subterranean dark/Has crossed the nadir, and begins to climb". It is the night, and it is death too. This shift is really the result of the remarkable central image of the poem, the "moon-eclipsing cone of night". Passing by the earth, the sun's rays cast a shadow which, because the sun is so much bigger than the earth, will taper off into space, the rays on all sides joining to produce a perfect cone of darkness. It is in this cone that the moon is eclipsed, and the earth wears it like a dunce's cap. It is this which we call night, towering because the sun is so far away, making the cone almost infinitely long. By producing in so few words such an almost tangible picture of what night is, and by giving us the apt and ironic metaphor of the foolscap, Housman suggests that night makes fools of us like death, and gives momentary shape to the formless emotions and associations that surround the experience of darkness, and the idea of death as the ultimate night. What it tends to make us sure of — whether it is true or not — is that this machinery is unchanging (it does not evolve) and that it always steadily turns.

It would be interesting to compare these two poems with one by Hardy, the well-known 'Drummer Hodge', which has much in common with 'Astronomy', besides being about the Boer War:

I

They throw in Drummer Hodge, to rest
　Uncoffined — just as found:
His landmark is a kopje-crest
　That breaks the veldt around;
And foreign constellations west
　Each night above his mound.

II

Young Hodge the Drummer never knew —
　Fresh from his Wessex home —
The meaning of the broad Karoo,
　The Bush, the dusty loam,
And why uprose to nightly view
　Strange stars amid the gloam.

III

Yet portion of that unknown plain
　Will Hodge forever be;
His homely Northern breast and brain
　Grow to some Southern tree,
And strange-eyed constellations reign
　His stars eternally.

The use of the stars as the major image of place is the significant shared feature of the two poems. But that feature also provides each of Hardy's stanzas with its closing couplet, just as the ground in which the Drummer lies provides the previous couplet, and this kind of repetitive structure is a trade-mark of Hardy's that finds no counterpart in the poems of Housman. What the stars produce here is a defamiliarising note. For both the land and its sky are strange to Drummer Hodge who, in contrast to the very active role taken by Herbert Housman in 'Astronomy', is a purely passive victim: he understands neither the land nor the sky above him, and he is thrown away like so much rubbish, past its use. This is possibly the first example in a recognisably modern tradition of anti-war poems; 'Astronomy', though it is about the tragedy of war, is not an anti-war poem as such. What points up the difference is the strong note of inhumanity in the opening lines of Hardy's poem. It has an earthy, bloody realism that Housman at all times avoids. It is an event on a human scale, with a body buried on a "kopje" or knoll, the "homely Northern breast and brain" dying under the eyes of strange constellations. As always with such protest at another's lot there is the danger of patronising the victim, who becomes just poor Drummer Hodge, too ignorant to know why the stars were different. In contrast, Herbert's quest "For pay and medals, name and rank" may have been vain, but it seems to be his responsibility. If he fails, it is because he has pitted himself not against an enemy of flesh and blood, but against the fixed and immutable cosmos itself — those allusions to navigation by the stars, and to the crucifix which have no equivalent in the apparently parallel imagery of the Hardy poem.

Yet the broad structure of each poem is the same. There is no mention of the enemy or the war; a soldier finds death in a foreign place — the same foreign place, as it happens — and the only concession made to any other actors in the piece is the first word in the Hardy poem, 'They', the disembodied plural who dispose of the dead Drummer. However, the two poetic events, (as opposed to the real events behind them) take place in different worlds. 'Astronomy', as said, pits the individual against his destiny; 'Drummer Hodge', on the other hand, is a more down-to-earth poem about alienation, the young man bred in Wessex is displaced, like a creature torn from one environmental set of conditions to another, becoming extinct. But this evolutionary nature wastes nothing; and whereas Housman's dead are scattered to the "twelve winds" (see *ASL* XXXII) that made them, in Hardy's poetry it is common for one form of life to be transformed into another, for Drummer Hodge to "Grow to some Southern tree".

I want to return to what Housman once said about the First World War making little difference, in his opinion, to anyone of imagination. Both men lived through the Great War, but as war poets they produced their most telling work in relation to the Boer War. It is a poetry with many important differences from World War I poetry; for instance, neither Hardy nor Housman had first-hand experience of war. Perhaps it is this fact which governs the absence of any description of the fighting: both poems we have looked at take very distant views, and one of the functions of the night sky in each is not so much to emphasise the dead man's separation from his homeland, as to point up our separation from him. They thus both leave us with an image of the man buried far away, for exile is more complete when even the body cannot be returned to its native soil. In this context it is interesting to read Hardy's lines. "Yet portion of that unknown plain/Will Hodge forever be" against Rupert Brooke's 'The Soldier': "there's some corner of a foreign field/That is forever England", which attempts to turn this exile into patriotic triumph. In complete contrast, and fittingly for a man whose poetic 'native soil' was very much a place of the imagination, the exile for Housman has little to do with actual topography. The change of orientation takes place on a larger, cosmic scale, as in 'Revolution', where night, rather than being just the sinking of the sun, is viewed from the perspective of the solar system as a movement in a vast mechanism. If one reads 'Revolution' as a political metaphor (although political poetry is a very rare species in Housman's work), it suggests a cyclical view of history rather similar to that developed by Yeats; much less complex, shorn of any occult significances, but still dominated by the figure of a vast wheel, and by the duality of day and night.

I want to dwell a little longer on the subject of A.E. Housman's war poetry (as opposed to his poetry of enlistment, which I take to be a rather separate subject) and discuss two poems which have caused some degree of controversy, in the attitude towards war and religion which they present – '1887' (*ASL* I) and 'Epitaph on an

Army of Mercenaries' (*LP* XXXVII). These two poems share exactly the same perspective on their subject, yet are separated by some twenty years, the first being a few years before the Boer War, the second being one of the poet's only creative responses to the Great War. Frank Harris, in his one disastrous meeting with Housman, praised '1887' for its anti-patriotic sentiments and got short shrift for it. What he did was to misread the nature of the irony in the poem, taking the play on the phrase "God save the Queen" as a debunking stance, and lines like "The saviours come not home to-night:/Themselves they could not save" as having a distinctly anti-war message behind them. But this is to miss the terms of the irony, which is directed not against the Queen but at God. The key to the reading comes in the third stanza:

> Now, when the flame they watch not towers
>   About the soil they trod,
> Lads, we'll remember friends of ours
>   Who shared the work with God.

It is the Jubilee, people are singing "God save the Queen" and remembering the dead of war, and the poet puts these two actions in stark relief to each other. If God does save the Queen, he has a lot of help: it is a fairly simple message, but it gains resonance through the rest of the poem, as in the two lines I quoted just now, which echo the Gospel of St. Mark XV 30 "Save thyself, and come down from the cross". This parallel between Christ and the soldier is one that Housman was to return to a number of times, and it lies behind the irony of the final stanza of the poem

> Oh, God will save her, fear you not:
>   Be you the men you've been,
> Get you the sons your fathers got,
>   And God will save the Queen.

To put it as succinctly as possible, God will not save the Queen directly, nor through the intercession of His son, but through the intercession of all the sons, the soldiers and sons of soldiers, because they are all Christs. As in 'Astronomy' they carry their cross to the supreme sacrifice.

'Epitaph on an Army of Mercenaries' takes this all one stage further, from the irony of 'God' working purely through the medium of the soldier (which suggests that if there were no soldier there would be, in *effect*, no God) to the bold statement that "What God abandoned, these defended,/And saved the sum of things for pay". Following the poems of enlistment, which focus on the young man signing up for "thirteen pence a day", this poem celebrates the deeds done by the professional soldier (not the privateer, which we tend to understand by the word "mercenary"). Again, 'Astronomy' is relevant, with its lines "For pay and medals, name and rank,/Things that he has not found" where the poet accepts that even his own brother's motivation for fighting was not the defence of a just cause. Although he is not an anti-war poet he does not indulge in any idealism in relation to war, and he does not demand that heroism should be a selfless sacrifice. In a very important sense it is all the more miraculous that the world (the poem puts it in these terms) can be saved by men ignorant, or innocent, of what they do:

> Their shoulders held the sky suspended;
> They stood, and earth's foundations stay;
> What God abandoned, these defended,
> And saved the sum of things for pay.

It is an atheistic poem, accepting the real motivations behind actions and celebrating them for their effects, rather than dismissing them as sordid. He manages to encapsulate this in the play of the word "sum", which at one and the same time and in the same action represents both the money they take and the whole of what they saved with their heroism. And of course, the lines *are* an epitaph. They have been paid what is throughout Housman's work the final reward for services rendered.

The Theory of a Scholar-Poet

Paul Naiditch has pointed out how little time and attention biographers have paid to Professor Housman's scholarship, in comparison to the important role it held in his life. In a book intended principally for those interested in his poetry, I have no chance to make amends for this, or do anything but tend to make the situation worse, but at least I can admit that it exists, and try to deal with some of the obvious prejudices which render the comments of most literary biographers and critics on the subject so misleading. Most comments follow along the lines of Auden's poem, "Deliberately he chose the dry-as-dust" and tend to see something self-defeating in his choice of a career, considering it a most unsuitable one for a poet. It's all a matter of putting the cart before the horses. Housman's passion for Jackson is judged to be the reason for his failure in Greats, and as a further reaction to lost love, and as a kind of a penance, he is presumed to have chosen textual criticism as his life's career (when surely, if he really did want to spite himself he could have made sure he spent the rest of his life in the Patent Office). The fact is that the one demonstrable reason for his performing worse than expected in his examinations is that he had already undertaken a course of work that sent him a long way off the track of the curriculum: he had started working on the manuscripts of his favourite Latin poet, Propertius. The only reason he could have taken to this at such an early stage, and in a way he must have known was likely to damage his university work and his future prospects, is that in some way he enjoyed the task.

Other factors in his career choice are found perplexing. It is said that he preferred Greek literature to Latin, yet chose Latin as his lifetime area of study because he said he "could not attain to eminence in both". But why Latin? Surely he was being perverse?

115

First, I don't know that his preference for Greek over Latin is at all a proven case. Secondly, such was the state of classical studies at the time that there was more opportunity for producing definitive textual work in Latin than in Greek. Thirdly, as Housman had to keep restating in published essays which literary people seem to only take half-seriously, in textual criticism matters of taste and aesthetics are irrelevant except in one vital area. When people ask why he chose the third-rate Manilius rather than Propertius as his life's work — a poet many would consider hardly worth editing — the only answer is that a real textual critic would not even ask the question. Housman saw quite clearly that, with new manuscript evidence having recently been discovered, there was the possibility of producing an edition of Manilius which would improve on the work of two of the greatest textual critics in history, Scaliger and Bentley, who had both produced editions of his tortuous and unreadable poem the *Astronomica*. The chance to be compared with these two demi-gods would be a true professional challenge. As for Propertius, in publishing in 1888 his 'Emendationes Propertianae' Housman wrote that he saw "no hope of completing a presentable commentary on Propertius within the next ten years", and thus effectively gave up his plans for such a work. His important series of articles on the manuscripts came out a few years later, but only as attempts at producing a suitable text, and without that commentary which would have been necessary, of course, for any full edition of the poet. In a sense it is fortunate that he did give up: his collation of the various manuscript sources and his subsequent recension or revision of them contains a serious flaw which did not come to light for some years, although there was a deal of criticism of the work at the time. The situation had, in fact, forced him to be rather too speculative, and he would have risked spending years on something only to see one day that he had been wasting his time. I like to think he suspected as much.

I have said that literary taste is irrelevant for the textual critic; the best way I can try to suggest this is ask you to imagine you are a car mechanic, presented with two cars, one a very comfortable and efficient saloon, the other a cheap pick-up truck. You will be able to drive one around for your own spare-time use and enjoyment, whilst working on the other; you merely have to decide which. Now, provided you have no professional interest in driving a pick-up truck, which one would you rather spend your life taking apart and putting back together, and which actually driving, now and then? Manilius may be the kind of pick-up truck nobody would really want to drive anyway, but from a mechanical point of view it is just another machine, potentially as rewarding to work on as any other. I think it might be difficult to know every single manuscript variation of a particular author and still find the work enjoyable to read.

Having said this there is one important area in which taste does play a part, I must briefly explain the work of the textual critic. First of all, classical texts come down to us through a process much like the game of Chinese whispers. It is a world devoid of authors' autographs; up until the medieval invention of printing, transmission of texts was purely the work of scribes, painstakingly copying text after text. These men — they would all be men — had two ways of making the life of the textual critic of later centuries difficult. They could make mistakes, transpose letters, skip lines, misspell or write what they thought they saw rather than what was actually there; but equally they could change things, perhaps finding a passage they could not make sense of (maybe because of an earlier corruption, or because of their own incapacity) and altering it until they could — in these days before the concept of copyright — 'improve' upon their author's work. Any mistake would of course have a knock-on effect down the line.

The transmission of a text would not, of course, go down a single line. One copy of a manuscript might itself be copied a number of times, each copy producing further manuscripts, each introducing their own variations. A diagram of such a process would look much like a family tree, and even more like the diagram of evolutionary descent produced by Darwin for his *Origin of Species*; a continual branching, but in this case including the possibility of two branches at some time coming together, that rare possibility of a scribe being influenced by two manuscripts. What is needed in order to do the job of a textual critic in this situation is a formidable grasp of the language and a minute study of all available relevant manuscripts (roughly, those eldest in each particular line of descent), as well as the following capabilities, described by Housman in his preface to *Manilius V* (1930):

> To read attentively, think correctly, omit no relevant consid-
> eration, and repress self-will, are not ordinary accomplishments;
> yet an emendator needs much more besides: just literary per-
> ception, congenial intimacy with the author, experience which
> must have been won by study, and mother wit which he must have
> brought from his mother's womb. (*P.&P.* p.393)

When it becomes clear that none of the extant manuscripts
contains the correct reading for a particular passage or line,
then something will have to be done to emend it. This may
be simple, if the corruptions are such that an obvious probable answer presents itself. But at all times one must think
whether or not the author would actually have written this. Is
it in her/his style or idiom; does it suit the context, not only
of the present passage, but of the work as a whole? At this point a
form of literary taste comes in. But it is a particular form of
literary taste or judgement, for you are aiming not at what you
yourself think is the right phrase, but what your author would
have chosen, an author from another culture, two or three thousand
years ago. If your author was not a terribly good poet anyway,
if he was Manilius, then you have to match your taste to his poor
taste.

What I have been describing could be looked at as a delicate piece
of detective or forensic work — I think it no coincidence that
Housman enjoyed detective fiction — and would probably give the
same kind of reward for painstaking labour. Not the apprehension
of a criminal, it is true (though the identification of a corrupt piece
of copyist's work may amount to the same thing), but a recon-
struction of the truth. The word truth plays an important role in
Housman's writings on textual criticism. Following it was, he
thought, the first duty of a critic. All this before a line of the
explanatory commentary, which requires another form of ency-
clopaedic knowledge, has been written. For instance, the extent of
Housman's comprehension of Roman astronomy and astrology is
displayed in the commentary to his text of Manilius, yet he would
have needed it in any case just to produce his recension of the text,
which is nothing more or less than a versified guide to the
constellations and planets and their use in the art of astrology, and
which contains many long sections which Housman correctly
described as being sums in verse. As a result of setting himself this

task Housman became probably the greatest authority on Roman astronomy and astrology of his day. The fact that he was interested in astronomy in the first place may have been another factor in attracting him to the *Astronomica*.

I want to move from an explanation of what textual criticism is to some account of Housman's attitude towards it. I think this is important, because he considered himself first and foremost a scholar and only secondly a poet. He did not think of himself as a literary critic at all; yet since he was involved, albeit fleetingly , in that discipline an adequate look at what he did call himself seems essential. In 1921 Housman delivered before the Classical Association in Cambridge a lecture called *The Application of Thought to Textual Criticism* (pub. 1922), a kind of manifesto for the type of textual work which he considered valid. The title is probably meant to be polemical, given that he seems to have thought most practitioners of textual criticism applied little or no thought to the matter; but the main drift of his argument is to run a course between what he saw as two dominant tendencies in the discipline. The one, practiced mainly by the English and emanating originally from Oxford in the mid-nineteenth century, saw textual criticism as a kind of extension of literary studies, with no real method at all. The other tendency was practiced almost exclusively in Germany, which with England made up the two great powers in classical studies, and consisted, as Housman saw it, in sacrificing intelligence for the maintenance of a rigid methodology, as if it were an exact science like mathematics. Housman's middle path ran as follows: "Textual criticism is a science, and, since it comprises of recension and emendation, it is also an art. It is the science of discovering error in texts and the art of removing it" (*P.&P.* p.325). He asserts that his profession is not a "sacred mystery": "We exercise textual criticism whenever we notice and correct a misprint. A man who possesses common sense and the use of reason must not expect to learn from treatises or lectures on textual criticism anything that he could not, with leisure and industry, find out for himself" (*P.&P.* p.325). Of course in reading this we must remember that Housman believed that common sense was less common that it ought to be; he also did believe that literary criticism was indeed something of a sacred mystery. Then, to dispose with the idea that it might be a "branch of mathematics", he says: "It deals with a matter not rigid and constant, like lines and numbers, but fluid and variable; namely the frailties and aberrations of the human mind, and of its insubordinate servants, the human fingers" (*P.&P.* pp.325–26).

This lays down the terms for what we could almost call an academic crusade, which Housman fought with the moral vigour of a political reformer. This is most obvious in his prefaces and reviews, where he lets his devastating wit loose on fellow academics who have failed to come up to his own high standards, which include honesty and endeavour, and the control of human vanity. Take this extended quote from a review of some work on Lucilius:

> But when Mr Marx and his school talk about 'audacia' they do not mean audacity, they mean alteration of the text; and they would be surprised to hear that the fabrication of imaginary contexts has any audacity about it. Just as murder is murder no longer if perpetrated by white men on black men or by patriots on kings; just as immorality exists in the relations on the sexes and nowhere else throughout the whole field of human conduct; so a conjecture is audacious when it is based on letters preserved in a MS., and ceases to be audacious, ceases even to be called a conjecture, when, like these conjectural supplements of Mr Marx's, it is based on nothing at all.
>
> (*SP* p.107)

The comparisons he makes in the middle of this passage are, I think, very illuminating; they are both political statements which might, in 1907, have sounded more in keeping from a liberal than the arch-conservative professor of Latin. Of course, we can now see how the comment on immorality hides a personal interest which none of his readers at the time would have had any clue to. The comment on white men killing black men, though straightforward Christian morality, might seem to be a strange one from a man always reckoned as a defender of the British Empire. After all, so much of the Empire came about through just this moral inconsistency. This is perhaps another case where we cannot take the stereotypical image of Housman the reactionary at face value. Both his atheism and his experience of his own sexuality must have led him to reappraise the moral conventions that surrounded him and, his own personal idiosyncrasies aside, to demand the same standard of common sense for them as for the sphere of textual studies. This is a sweeping generalisation, I know, but I think it can make sense of his having apparently recorded a casting vote in favour of votes for women (see p. 55 above). Temperamentally he was misogynistic, but perhaps he had enough maturity to separate temperament from politics. The light-hearted tone of his jibes at Laurence's politics in letters to him suggests as much.

What may seem less than commonsensical is the moral fervour with which he attacked the issues of textual criticism, almost as if they were as important as the issues he used as examples. To him, as a professional amongst other professionals, perhaps they were. We can only read such work out of context, for it was never intended for the lay person at all, but takes place in the atmosphere of in-fighting between the members of a very exclusive and elitist club. There was a tradition of bitchiness in this club, albeit one that Housman was instrumental in trying to revive, and it is quite clear that he enjoyed calling a fool a fool. There is a notorious list amongst his papers which consists of a large number of barbed comments with gaps where names could be fitted, usually considered to be a kind of store of ammunition, waiting for the next unfortunate victim. This has been accused of being bad form on his behalf, as if the only way to be honestly withering is to be spontaneously so. But when they turn up, they always fit the victim as if they *were* spontaneous, which is surely what matters. They were produced for effect, to drive home his point about the shortcomings of somebody's work with a barbed piece of humour. He was often cruel, and felt justified in being so when somebody's academic vanity threatened to distort or hide the truth. But if we accept that, we cannot really expect that he should only be cruel off-the-cuff. Here are a few examples of this cruelty, from his published work:

> They say that he was born of human parentage; but if so he must have been suckled by Caucasian tigers.***Not only had Jacob no sense for grammar, no sense for coherency, no sense for sense, but being himself possessed by a passion for the clumsy and the hispid he imputed this disgusting taste to all the authors whom he edited; and Manilius, the one Latin poet who excels even Ovid in verbal point and smartness, is accordingly constrained to write the sort of poetry which might have been composed by Nebuchadnezzar when he was driven from men and did eat grass as oxen.
>
> (*SP* 33)

> The corrections of Ellis were rather more numerous, and one or two of them were very pretty, but his readers were in perpetual contact with the intellect of an idiot child . . . (*SP* 45)

> . . . the Lachmanns and Madvigs are gone, the Mosers and Forbigers remain; and now they lift up their heads and rejoice aloud at the emancipation of human incapacity. (*SP* 41)

This is not exactly the way to win friends, but it influenced people. Housman did not make such comments without very good reason, and his arguments are always lucid and fair, taking care to deal with any points which may be made, or had been made, against him. Overall he was as good a judge of his own faults as of other people's, and he could forgive honest mistakes; what he could not forgive was laziness or dishonesty. Unfortunately he found many of his contemporaries built of one or other of these at some time in his career, even some of those who had written testimonials on his behalf for the U.C.L. professorship. Robinson Ellis, the "idiot child", was one of these: he had referred to the candidate in his letter of recommendation as "an amiable and modest man". When Housman pronounced his judgment Ellis was already long dead. There was some concession made to the feelings of those whom Housman was personally acquainted with, but not much. It has been said that it was fortunate that testimonials were not required for the Kennedy Professorship at Cambridge, and it was probably was.

Through his controversial writings, Housman gained a reputation as a Germanophobe, and this delayed the recognition of his own talents in that country by a number of years. The reason for this is fairly straightforward: he considered that the most damaging trend in textual criticism around the turn of the century was the modern German school's almost exclusive reliance on method over and above the power of reason:

> Whenever you see a writer's practice praised as *methodisch*, you find upon investigation that he has laid down a hard and fast rule and has stuck to it through thick and thin. Whenever you see a writer's practice blamed as *willkürlich* [arbitrary], you find upon investigation that he has been guilty of the high crime and misdemeanour of reasoning. (*P.&P.* p.308)

This has to be read in the context of his comments about any "hard and fast" laws in relation to criticism:

> A man who never violates the laws of criticism is no critic. The laws of criticism are nothing but a string of generalisations, necessarily inaccurate, which have been framed by the benevolent for the guidance, the support, and the restraint, of three classes of persons. They are leading strings for infants, they are crutches for cripples and they are strait-waistcoats for maniacs. (*P.&P.* p.309)

In addition to these three, he invented a few other classes of persons to which he consigned professional critics who slavishly laid down such false commandments. These were the "conservative critics" who tended to oppose the use of conjecture and find tortuous interpretations for text which Housman could only consider corrupt, since one of their laws tended to be to find a "best manuscript" and to support its readings in the teeth of all others. He saw this as not only wrong, not only lazy, but a betrayal of one's scholarly duty to seek the truth. He could be quite literally damning:

> indeed I imagine that Mr Buecheler, when he first perused Mr Sudhaus' edition of the *Aetna*, must have felt something like Sin when she gave birth to Death. (*SP* p.44)

Anybody who could produce this invective was not going to win any prizes for international diplomacy; but xenophobia was not one of Housman's character traits. In fact he believed that for most of the nineteenth century Germany had been the world leader in the field of textual criticism, and that insights into its scientific aspects from Lachmann, Madvig and Rischl were the most significant advances of their age. But he also thought that these insights had been ossified into laws, whilst the actual practice of these pre-eminent masters had been largely ignored by a less talented generation of academics. He blamed the unification of Germany under Bismarck for leading the brightest of German youth away from the universities and into the expanding arenas of industry and politics. It was a matter of circumstance, historical and political, but not of race:

> Patriotism has a great name as a virtue, and in civic matters, at the
> present stage of the world's history, it possibly still does more
> good than harm; but in the sphere of the intellect it is an
> unmitigated nuisance. I do not know which cuts the worse figure:
> a German scholar encouraging his countrymen to believe that 'wir
> Deutsche' have nothing to learn from foreigners, or an English-
> man demonstrating the unity of Homer by sneers at 'Teutonic
> professors', who are supposed by his audience to have goggle eyes
> behind large spectacles, and ragged moustaches saturated in lager
> beer, and consequently to be incapable of forming literary
> judgments. (*SP* pp.135–36)

It is another of the paradoxes of Housman's character that
while he seemed to have carried about his own fair share
of prejudice, in terms of work he not only condemned prejudice of all kinds but could see the insidious way it operated.
He knew that even in the field of the intellect fashion functioned
in a prejudicial way, leading people to praise writers whose
work upheld their own ready-made assumptions, and to dismiss
work which challenged those assumptions. The reasoning behind the work would tend to be ignored, and the weight of
interest would fall upon the conclusions no matter how they
were formulated. Naturally Housman had a better way of putting
it:

> Stand on a barrel in the streets of Baghdad, and say in a loud voice,
> 'Twice two is four, and ginger is hot in the mouth, therefore
> Mohammed is the prophet of God', and your logic will probably
> escape criticism; or, if anyone by chance should criticise it, you
> could easily silence him by calling him a Christian dog. (*SP* p.136)

This could give us another insight into his atheism. Transpose the
passage from an Islamic to a Christian context and ask how
common this kind of reasoning would have been in the Church of
England Housman knew ("Spring comes, the cuckoo calls in the
woods, Christ is . . ."). There is more of Housman in these
'pedantic' studies (as he used to call them) than he liked to let on.
   I want to end this apparent digression, which I hope has
conveyed at least something of the atmosphere in which A.E.
Housman conducted his day-to-day business, and move from
textual criticism to literary criticism. Housman did not claim to be

a literary critic, in fact he thought that literary critics were rarer than great poets. This may sound absurd, especially as his Leslie Stephen Lecture *The Name and Nature of Poetry* is nothing more nor less than a piece of literary criticism itself. But what he meant by the term and what we would understand by it, living in an age when literary studies have become not so much a discipline as an industry, are two different things. "Orators and poets, sages and saints and heroes, if rare in comparison with blackberries, are yet commoner than the appearance of Halley's comet; literary critics are less common (*P.&P.* p.302). He set high standards:

> By a literary critic I understand a man who has things to say about literature which are both true and new. Appreciation of literature, and the ability to say things about it which are true but not new, is a much commoner endowment. That a scholar should appreciate literature is good for his own pleasure and profit; but it is none of his business to communicate that appreciation to his audience. Appreciation of literature is just as likely to be found in his audience as in him, for it has no connexion with scholarship. (*P.&P.* p.302–3)

Matthew Arnold "the great critic of our land and time" was Housman's idea of what a literary critic should be. Arnold it was whose 'Empedocles on Etna' the undergraduate Housman considered contained "all the law and the prophets" — all that is worth knowing, that is to say — and in criticism Housman stood for the originality of thought twinned with clarity of expression which is also the hallmark of his own best prose. The criticism that he wrote he considered to be no more than evidence of his appreciation of literature, and (although his paper on Swinburne and the first couple of pages of one on Arnold do survive) it consisted almost exclusively of occasional papers written mainly for the University College London literary society and destroyed after his death. The only exception is *The Name and Nature of Poetry*, which could therefore be called his only piece of 'professional' literary criticism, and the only one he intended to outlive him.

It is therefore quite in keeping that he should begin the lecture with a disclaimer, indicating that his writing it does not mean that he now considers himself a critic. His recreational reading of "the best literature of several languages" may have mellowed his personal opinions:

> But personal opinions they remain, not truths to be imparted as such with the sureness of superior insight and knowledge. I hope however that for brevity's sake, and your own, you will accept the disclaimer once for all, and that when hereafter I may say that things are thus or thus, you will not insist on my saying instead that I humbly venture to conceive them so or that I diffidently offer the suggestion to your better judgment. (*P.&P.* p.350)

This statement is usually effectively ignored by those who comment on the essay, but I think that it does have importance. Anyone who reads his prefaces and classical reviews is used to the magisterial tone of Housman's address, and to the absolute confidence with which he put forward argument and opinion. Here is something he presented with much less confidence, and the trouble it gave him in the writing also suggests a man struggling with unfamiliar material. Housman said that he always found English prose a struggle to write (whereas he found poetry either easy or impossible), but *The Name and Nature of Poetry* appears, because of its subject, to have been particularly taxing. He admits that his first idea had been to write on 'The Artifice of Versification', elucidating the "natural laws by which all versification is conditioned" (p. 350), but this would naturally have made a rather dry lecture. So he went for something rather more ambitious, nothing more or less than an attempt to define what, for him, poetry actually is.

Since it is given to us as a personal statement, I want to discuss the major features of this critical Housmanian manifesto in relation to his own poetry, trying to see how much his poetry and theory interact. As I have shown, for a diffident piece of work it certainly caused a deal of controversy at the time; deliberately so, I believe, since nobody as well-read and well-informed as Housman could have been unaware that it would be taken as a direct challenge to rising Cambridge critics of the time — including I.A. Richards and F.R. Leavis — in whose own back yard he had pitched his soap-box. To that extent his disclaimer is not only honest but on another level deeply ironic: he didn't think he was a critic, but I doubt he would have awarded any of them the coveted title either.

'Poetry is not the thing said but a way of saying it.' There is, for Housman, an absolute separability of form and content on this level. But it is not form and content as usually understood. Early in the lecture he is careful to point out the difference he understands between poetry and verse, the former being verse "which can at least be called literature, though it may differ from prose only in its metrical form," (p.351); poetry as 'a way of saying it' is a different order of form. It is the words very much in their music as opposed to their sense: poetry can be meaningless. Conversely, what people call poetry can be devoid of all true poetic form. The seventeenth century Metaphysical poets belonged to a time "in which the place of poetry was usurped by something very different which possessed the proper and specific name of wit" — wit in Johnson's definition as "a combination of dissimilar images, or discovery of occult resemblances in things apparently unlike". It is in this context that Housman makes a comment that has been frequently misinterpreted: "Simile and metaphor, *things inessential to poetry*, were their great and engrossing pre-occupation, and were prized the more in proportion as they were further fetched" (p.353; my italics). Housman has been taken to imply here that he is somehow against the use of simile and metaphor in poetry; and when it can be pointed out that some of his best poetry is intensely metaphorical, he seems to have been caught out contradicting himself. After all, even such a characteristic and famous Shropshire Lad poem as 'Loveliest of trees, the cherry now' (*ASL* II), and which incidentally has caused numerous cherry trees to be planted in the poet's honour, ends with a metaphorical description of the blossom: "About the woodlands I will go/To see the cherry hung with snow".

But what Housman was objecting to was not the presence of metaphor *in* poetry, but the mistaking of metaphor *for* poetry. Since metaphor and simile can just as easily be found in prose, they cannot be a factor of the thing that makes poetry different from prose (and from verse): they are therefore inessential to it. Housman is of course setting himself against any theory of poetic language which grounds itself in metaphor: it may be part of the thing said, but it is not part of the way of saying it.

The eighteenth century is accused of producing sham poetry, a deliberate counterfeit. The poetic diction devised under the influence of Dryden both as ornament and as a measure of correctness, "consisted in always using the wrong word instead of the right." Such a rigid idea of what constituted poetic language had according to Housman far-reaching consequences:

A thick, stiff unaccommodating medium was interposed between the writer and his work. And this deadening of language had a consequence beyond its own sphere: its effects worked inward, and deadened perception. That which could no longer be described was no longer noticed. (p.357)

Despite this, Housman can praise passages of Dryden's poetry and say of Pope that "perhaps no English poem of greater than lyric length, . . . , is quite so perfect as *The Rape of the Lock*". But overall the century is characterised as one of the intelligence, not of poetic emotion, so that its literature is "an admirable and most enjoyable thing", although incapable of reaching the true heights:

> . . . the special task and characteristic achievement of the age was the invention and establishment of a healthy, workmanlike, athletic prose, to supersede the cumbrous and decorated and self-admiring prose of a Milton or a Jeremy Taylor, and to become a trustworthy implement for accurate thinking and the serious pursuit of truth . . .. (p.355)

Housman uses the seventeenth and eighteenth centuries not so much as Aunt Sallys as exemplars in the development of his definition of the essentially poetic element in literature; the one representing the mistaking of something else for poetry, the other the substitution of a counterfeit in the form of a rigid set of conventions. This element is something above and beyond his earlier statement of what poetry is generally expected to be, namely, verse which can at least be called 'literature'. It appears that the literary and the poetic are almost separate entities, and that though all poetry is by definition literature, the literary element within it forms a kind of alloy with the poetic essence:

> The writing of poetry proceeded, and much of the poetry written was excellent literature; but excellent literature which is also poetry is not therefore excellent poetry, and the poetry of the eighteenth century was most satisfactory when it did not try to be poetical.
>
> (pp.355–56)

This of course brings up the question, is there a pure poetry, and what might that be? Again it is one that Housman moves towards slowly, by example, producing along the way perhaps his most startling statement. He takes the following simple, almost naive lines by Dr Watts:

> Soft and easy is thy cradle,
>   Coarse and hard thy Saviour lay,
> When his birthplace was a stable
>   And his softest bed was hay.

"That simple verse", he says, "bad rhyme and all, is poetry beyond Pope". As a rather irrational disparagement of Pope this would be one thing; but Housman has already talked of *The Rape of the Lock* in terms of perfection, comparing it with work by Coleridge and Chaucer. Did he think that Dr Watts was a better poet than Coleridge and Chaucer? Fortunately not, although it would be easier for us if he had. Again, his qualification is important: the poems he had previously compared with Pope's masterpiece were all of "greater than lyric length". Housman clearly had in his mind a definition of poetry based upon the lyric, the short, self-enclosed single poetic utterance. The problem with the longer poem is that in order to sustain itself it needs to integrate aspects of literature which are not, in Housman's terms, essentially poetic, such as narrative, argument, dramatic structure: more and more of alloy into the basic poetic ingredient. Clearly too much of this weakens the poetic force of the work.

The verse by Dr Watts is chosen because of its simplicity, because there is little to distract the mind's attention from the clarity, not of the meaning but of the language. For Housman there has to be that distinction. In other words the poetic element in a work is independent of meaning and can, at least in theory, survive without it. Watts's verse is saying something, but it is saying very little; the versification can be found to be at fault — there is a "bad rhyme" of cradle with stable — but the effect on Housman is poetry. So what is the poetic, if it has nothing to do with the meaning and is independent, at least to some extent, of the quality of versification or of the purely auditory function of the work? Housman continues to answer the question by a process very much like evading the issue, finding more things that can be pared away and yet leave poetry intact.

The next is sanity. He finds that there were four true poets in the eighteenth century 'Age of Reason'. They had one thing in common. "They were mad". Again, it is not madness as a positive attribute that Housman sees as being an issue here. It is not so much what their minds were capable of but what they were incapable of: "elements of their nature were more or less insurgent against the centralised tyranny of the intellect, and their brains were not thrones on which the great usurper could sit secure" (p. 365). The metaphor he uses here says it all; in an age of Reason, madness becomes a form of insurrection. Not that they chose it, but they did choose in their poetry to work against the grain of reason and the intellect. These four — Collins, Smart, Cowper and Blake — all have something else in common; their poetry was not rated highly by their eighteenth century contemporaries, and they are all best read in the context of the Romantic tradition which followed them, the tradition of which Housman was one of the last members. Blake, of course, is often considered the first romantic poet, so much of its individualism seeming to stem from his rereading of the character of Milton's Satan from *Paradise Lost* in his *The Marriage of Heaven and Hell*. But this is not the Blake that interests A.E.H:

> For me the most poetical of all poets is Blake. I find his lyrical note as beautiful as Shakespeare's and more beautiful than anyone else's; and I call him more poetical than Shakespeare, even though Shakespeare has so much more poetry, because poetry in him preponderates more than in Shakespeare over everything else, and instead of being confounded in a great river can be drunk pure from a slender channel of its own. (pp.365–66)

Some have inferred from this that he preferred Blake to Shakespeare, or considered him a greater poet. Neither of these ideas is strictly true. The "everything else", the alloy, as I have been calling it, can strengthen the work it appears in, make it better literature and its author a better writer. But it can also weaken the amalgam, as he suggested it does with the worst parts of Shakespeare. Blake "gives us poetry neat, or unadulterated with so little meaning that nothing except poetic emotion is perceived and matters" (p.366).

Poetic emotion, which seems to be something other than the emotion inherent in the meaning of a text — its tragedy, for instance — is something independent of context. "Neat" or "pure" poetry is something Blake achieves again and again, Shakespeare "now and then", yet the most famous example of it which Housman gives is a song of Shakespeare's:

> Take O take those lips away
>   That so sweetly were forsworn,
> And those eyes, the break of day,
>   Lights that do mislead the morn;
> But my kisses bring again
>   bring again,
> Seals of love, but seal'd in vain,
>   seal'd in vain.

Housman's comment: "This is nonsense; but it is ravishing poetry" (p.366). But apparently Shakespeare could achieve the same effect when he "fills such poetry with thought", so that songs like 'Fear no more the heat o' the sun' and 'O mistress mine, where are you roaming' are the very summits of lyrical achievement, they are "indeed greater and more moving poems, but I hardly know how to call them more poetical" (p.366). This is Housman's Shakespeare, not the writer of the great soliloquies, not the author of the sonnets, not the creator of the archetypal tragic figures of the English stage, Hamlet and Lear and Macbeth; in fact not the dramatist at all but the writer of perfection in miniature. And of course the songs of Shakespeare are one of the few influences Housman admitted to. His Blake was also a very edited version, the poet of the *Songs of Innocence and of Experience* and various miscellaneous and notebook poems, but certainly not the writer of the prophetic books. Before quoting from 'My Spectre around me night and day' he wrote that these verses "probably possessed for Blake a meaning, and his students think that they have found it; but the meaning is a poor foolish disappointing thing in comparison with the verses themselves" (p.367). Prophesy is all about interpretation and Housman is in essence denying that interpretation has anything to do with the poetic.

> Tho' thou art worship'd by the names divine
>   Of Jesus and Jehovah, thou art still

> The Son of Morn in weary Night's decline,
> The lost traveller's dream under the hill.

"It purports to be theology: what theological sense, if any, it may have, I cannot imagine and feel no wish to learn: it is pure and self-existent poetry, which leaves no room in me for anything besides" (pp.368–69). What seems to be present in this verse, if it isn't sense, is a gesture, and a sad and rather plaintive one. All of Housman's examples of pure poetry either embody or end on this note, this often inexplicable sense of sadness and loss. When he actually gets closest to explaining the effect of pure poetry, it is in these terms that he attempts his explanation:

> Nymphs and shepherds, dance no more —
>
> what is it that can draw tears, as I know it can, to the eyes of more than one? What in the world is there to cry about? Why have the mere words the physical effect of pathos when the sense of the passage is blithe and gay? I can only say, because they are poetry, and find their way to something in man which is obscure and latent, something older than the present organisation of his nature, like the patches of fen which still linger here and there in the drained lands of Cambridgeshire. (p.369)

This smacks of a sentimentalist definition of poetry. After all, we know Housman was fond of melodrama, and he made some surprisingly good use of it in his poems. He may have gone further and made sentiment, a contextless self-existent sentiment, the very basis for his poetry. But as if sensing this possible conclusion he immediately forestalls it. His very next sentence is: "Poetry indeed seems to me more physical than intellectual". What are we to make of this? It is almost as if he were teasing us, leading us to the very root of what he has called "poetic emotion" and just before we grasp what he means, pointing us to something completely different:

> Experience has taught me, when I am shaving of a morning, to keep watch over my thoughts, because, if a line of poetry strays into my memory, my skin bristles so that the razor ceases to act. This particular symptom is accompanied by a shiver down the spine; there is another which consists in a constriction of the throat and a precipitation of water to the eyes; and there is a third

which I can only describe by borrowing a phrase from one of
Keats's last letters, where he says, speaking of Fanny Brawne,
'everything that reminds me of her goes through me like a spear.'
The seat of this sensation is the pit of the stomach. (p.369–70)

There are times when you read something written for public
oration and wish very sincerely that you could have been there to
see it delivered by its author. For me this is one of them. How
would Housman have spoken this passage: with affected sincerity,
matter-of-factly, or with a twinkle in the eye? We all (I presume)
know something of the shiver down the spine, a sensation which
usually has different triggers for different people, and no doubt for
some people poetry can be such a trigger. Certain coincidences of
timbre and note-value in music might be one common example. It
is a sensation which could perhaps be described as bordering
between the physical and the emotional. It tends to come out
of the blue and has no real connection with memory or anything
we intellectually understand about the situation in which it
happens. It tends to be very brief. Now I do not want to deny that
Housman had the experience he describes in this passage, or that it
may have been quite a common one. Though I do feel a bit
suspicious at the thought of Housman clutching his throat and
cursing Coleridge, which is the kind of thing the passage suggests
to me.

Yet there must be something more behind this. In the ubiquitous
letter to Maurice Pollet he writes, "I did not begin to write poetry
in earnest until the really emotional part of my life was over; and my
poetry, so far as I could make out, sprang chiefly from physical
conditions, such as a relaxed sore throat during my most prolific
period, the first five months of 1895" (*P.&P.* p.469). This is a fairly
remarkable claim, but here is not the only place that he made it, so
we can presume there is at least some truth in it. Maybe the
emotional part of his life had indeed ended, but the poems seem to
be all about the repercussions of that emotional life, which suggests
to me that it was only ended because it was finding an outlet in his
writing. A sore throat lasting for five months is a pretty rare
phenomenon. It is again possible (one can say no more) that this
was a physical symptom with psychological origins, a result of the
psychical pressure that Housman was actually under, the result of
repression.

But what I think has happened here is that Housman has played an intellectual game with us. Knowing he was no critic he set himself a task which the very greatest critics he knew had failed in, namely, to define poetry. He goes through with an argument which is a constant act of deferring the answer; he talks of the difference between verse and poetry, between poetry and other literature, between sense and non-sense, leading us on to expect some kind of universal definition of what he considers the essence of poetry. He has already told us that it has nothing to do with the intellect; now he ruthlessly carries through the logic of his argument and refuses to make his answer intellectual. He produces an academic essay, full of sweeping and (despite his disclaimers) authoritative judgments on the poetry of three centuries and virtually ends it all by saying, "It is so because I feel it in the pit of my stomach". He has avoided playing the literary critic because he has avoided making anything but a purely personal statement.

As I said, I do not want to deny that physical symptoms of the kind described did occur in Housman. But the way he presents them strikes me as very interesting. The careful, pedantic description is almost comic: "precipitation of water to the eyes" — isn't this a little stilted; and isn't the reference to dying Keats writing of Fanny Brawne rather over the top? I say this because something in the passage reminds me of a piece of writing Housman once claimed he carried around with him "as a sort of intellectual salvolatile". He quotes it in the remaining fragment of his essay on Matthew Arnold (*P.&P.* pp.275–76) as an amusing and invigorating example of bad criticism, from the *Daily Chronicle*, April 17, 1888; it purports to be about Arnold's poetry:

> His muse mounted upwards with bright thoughts, as the skylark shakes dewdrops from its wings as it carols at 'Heaven's Gate', or like a mountain brooklet carrying many a wildflower on its wavelets, his melody flowed cheerily on. Sometimes too his music rises like that of the mysterious ocean casting up pearls as it rolls.

To this stuff, Housman replies:

> Now at last I hope you have a clear conception of the real Matthew Arnold: now you will be able to recognise his poetry when you come across it; and no doubt you will easily distinguish between his three poetical manners, — that in which he shakes the dewdrops from his wing, that in which he carries wildflowers on his wavelets, and that in which he casts up pearls as he rolls.

And now, perhaps you too can recognise the essence of poetry and distinguish *its* three forms, — that in which it sends shivers down the spine, that in which it constricts the throat and precipitates water to the eyes, and that in which the pit of your stomach makes you feel like Keats thinking of Fanny Brawne or having a spear go through you. The piece about Arnold is ridiculous because it is so heavily metaphorical that the subject is lost behind a curtain of twee images. Housman's piece is so personal and physiological that the subject is lost in something between hayfever and a hangover. Somebody as intellectually rigorous as Professor Housman would surely realise that, and would only be doing it for a reason. I think the joke was meant to be on the so-called (as Housman would see them) critics in his audience, people trying to intellectualise the pursuit of poetry being given the runaround by somebody saying, in effect, 'poems are poems'.

If you look at Housman's essay for the essence of poetry all you find are indeed a series of negatives, behind which the answer is always an absence. So either there is no 'Name and Nature of Poetry' or else it defies definition. But logically, if we can't define it, we can't be sure it exists anyway, you can merely believe in it. I wonder whether he realised that and provided, in the 'shaving scene', a kind of *reductio ad absurduam* of the whole enterprise. As a critic or scholar, of course, he could never have got away with it; but he was a poet too, and his very next move was to admit that he was 'tinged' or 'tainted' by coming to poetry from two sides: reader and writer. Using the previous passage as the switch from the academic to the personal and artistic he now produces his famous explanation of his own writing experience, that "in its first stage" the production of a poem "is less an active than a passive and involuntary process". He goes on, "if I were obliged, not to define poetry, but to name the class of things to which it belongs, I should call it a secretion; whether a natural secretion, like turpentine in the fir, or a morbid secretion, like the pearl in the oyster" (p.370). His own

135

case, he admits, is the latter, "though I may not deal with the material so cleverly as the oyster does". Interestingly his next comment, that "I have seldom written poetry unless I was rather out of health, and the experience, though pleasurable, was generally agitating and exhausting", gained approval from, of all people, T. S. Eliot. "I believe that I understand that sentence," he wrote, after saying that Housman's description of his own writing experience recounted "the authentic processes of a real poet". This description recounts the nature of the secretion: the pint of beer at lunch; the long afternoon walk during which lines of poetry "would flow into my mind, with sudden and unaccountable emotion"; the going home to record the odd lines and stanzas, leaving gaps, in the hope "that further inspiration" might be forthcoming another day; and when it wasn't, the "matter of trouble and anxiety" when it had to be "taken in hand and completed by the brain". He even ends by teasing his audience, and the literary critics who have come to his poetry since, by saying how the last poem in *A Shropshire Lad* is a fair example of all stages of this process. Two stanzas came straight into his head (he even says which part of London he was walking through), a third appearing, "with a little coaxing after tea", and the fourth being left to the brain, needing to be written out thirteen times and taking over a year. Only, he never tells us which stanzas are which, and for some reason the notebook drafts for that poem do not survive.

★

Perhaps we can backtrack to Housman's comments on Shakespeare. The influence of the songs on his poetry is important because it forms a very real link between his writing practice and his theory as propounded in *The Name and Nature of Poetry*. Now Housman never wrote nonsense in the way that he calls 'Take O take those lips away' nonsense. In fact he did write a considerable amount of nonsense-verse, but that is of another order and irrelevant here. Of course it would be possible to argue that in the context of its appearance in *Measure for Measure* the song does have meaning; but Housman is considering it as a song, an independent lyric, shorn of its literary but non-poetical setting. In this sense it is indeed difficult to distil anything like a paraphraseable meaning from the poem, although its beauty and emotional intensity are, I think, beyond reasonable doubt. Nothing in Housman approaches it in style, nor does he allude to it in any of his poems. But one of the songs he mentions in the Leslie Stephen Lecture 'Fear no more the heat o' the sun' does appear. In Fletcher's list of "reminiscences" four out of the fifteen echoes of Shakespeare come from this one song from *Cymbeline*, more than any other single poem or play. It is a funeral song, with the same emotional tone of plaintive sadness that is to be found in Housman's examples of "pure" poetry. But rather like the stanza by Dr Watts, it is not saying very much: "Fear no more", you are dead and nobody and nothing can harm you. It is a theme not uncommon to Housman.

It finds its way into consecutive poems in *A Shropshire Lad*, 'The Immortal Part' and 'Shot? so quick, so clean an ending?' (*ASL* XLIII & XLIV), poems which not only follow each other but take two very different perspectives on death. 'Fear the heat o' the sun no more', say the bones in the first poem, tempting the flesh with death, in favour of their own 'birth'. The latter poem echoes three lines of the song:

> . . . Home art gone and ta'en thy wages.
> Golden lads and girls all must,
> As chimney-sweepers, come to dust.

"Come to dust" is also the refrain which ends each of the first three stanzas (the fourth is more of a chant warding off evil, rather than part of the song as such). Housman conflates this into two lines: "Dust's your wages, son of sorrow,/But men may come to worse than dust", i.e. to shame, dishonour, harm to others, things referred to in the *Cymbeline* song: "Fear not slander, censure rash;/ Thou hast finish'd joy and moan". It seems very significant that two such contrasting poems about death, placed side by side in the volume, should also make reference to the same Shakespeare funeral song. 'The Immortal Part' is a work with quite a sinister tone, death being the relentless force which brings birth and victory to the 'immortal' bones, whereas the verses about the Woolwich Cadet are very much verses of consolation. "Fear no more the heat o' the sun" actually embodies a similar sense of contradiction or paradox. It is presented as an antiphonal song, sung by Guiderius and Arviragus over the body of Imogen (who turns out not to be dead) and partly in honour of Cloten, whom Guiderius has killed and whose head he has just carried in. So the song, beautiful and straightforward as it is, actually presents itself in a context shot through with ambiguity, as when Imogen awakes alone with the headless body of Cloten, sees him dressed in her husband's clothes and thinks he is her husband, the ironically-named Posthumus. She even curses Cloten as being one she presumes guilty of the murder.

What can all this mean for our reading of Housman? We already know that the Woolwich Cadet poem has a hidden context; the poet himself knows at first hand the kind of moral dilemma which the subject of his poem found the ultimate answer to. But it is not his own answer. Perhaps — only perhaps — the poet is praising the cadet for a courage he knows he has not got, and which he envies. He too has a "household traitor" which he does not kill. And don't the bones in 'The Immortal Part' also represent a "household traitor"? Behind the obvious signification we could possibly see the bones as evoking a force which feeds off another kind of death, this time a moral death. The bones do not suggest that the death they require is any kind of protection from shame. All this would tend to reinforce what I have said earlier about the Woolwich Cadet poem being the obverse of the indignant verse about Oscar Wilde, showing Housman at his most guilt-ridden in the face of his sexuality, exalting the young soldier as a paragon of what an upstanding Victorian should really do, when placed in such a dire moral dilemma.

In saying this, of course, I am flying in the face of claims made by the poet in *The Name and Nature of Poetry*. From that we should expect that the influence of Shakespeare's songs on his poetry will have nothing to do with such non-poetical material as dramatic structure and irony. But Housman knew and admitted that there was more to poetry than the purely poetical he dangles tantalisingly before us in his Leslie Stephen Lecture. He had good reason, however, to believe in such an essence, even though he realised the impossibility of demonstrating its existence intellectually. If poetry were inextricably bound up with the context in which it was written, and the meanings in and behind it, then his own work would depend very much on the personal and psychological forces working, as it were, under cover. He told Moses Jackson that he was largely responsible for the poetry, but this fact, and the love and the desire behind it, were necessarily cloaked by the texture of the poems themselves, and are identifiable only, for the most part, through gaps in the texts and through the deeper associations they call up. The notion of 'Pure Poetry' is perhaps one attempt to save his art from being totally dependent upon this whole complex of pain, frustration and shame, as well as joy and love. I feel that breaking through all the disguises makes Housman a better and (for this age at least) more important poet.

But returning to poetic surfaces, Shakespeare surely had an important influence on Housman's style, parallel to the one exercised by Heine. The simplicity of language which is not only one of the chief beauties of Shakespeare's songs, but which also acts as such a foil for the complex dramatic and emotional situations into which they are inserted, is something which the Victorian poet seems to have made his own second nature. Few poets in the English language have been as skillful in their use of the monosyllabic line, the deft manipulation of tone and pace among units of apparently the same length. The point is to realise that monosyllabic words are not all of the same length; after that, the possibilities for creating sound patterns amongst them become almost numberless. I want to look at a single stanza from *ASL* XXXVI, the first:

> White in the moon the long road lies,
> The moon stands blank above;
> White in the moon the long road lies
> That leads me from my love.

Every word but one here has just one syllable, and the four lines amount to a subtle play between simplicity and obviousness of vocabulary and the texture of sound and rhythm. It pays to read the stanza slowly, aloud, letting the sounds roll over the tongue. At first glance it seems almost to pass below the level of critical comment; again, it is saying very little, and saying it in an apparently unremarkable way. Indeed, the verse seems as flat and straight as the road it describes, and the image of the white road in the moonlight is almost a cliché. But I think there is something haunting about the lines, and it may pay to make some attempt to explain it.

The repeated first and third line is deliberately drawn out — eight syllables, five of them stresses: "White in the moon the long road lies". This tends, of course, to complement the idea of the endless road, whilst the repetition, particularly in the word "moon", could be called mesmerising. The patterning of vowel sounds in the stanza is dominated by a play on the letter 'O', varying it from the long double in the thrice-repeated "moon", through "long" and "road" to the shorter sound in the rhyme words "above" and "love". Because of the repetition each variation on this vowel-sound occurs in just one word, except for the last, shared by the disyllabic "above" and the final, most significant word "love". So the ear is given a play of subtle variations to take in amongst the apparent monotony, a play which culminates in "love". A similar development could be argued for in the alliterative sequence of long/lies/long/lies/leads/love. Also, in what sense does the road lie? The word is drummed home, whilst in the context of the poem the straightness of the road promises return, the straight route round the globe.

Then there is the second line. If there is one surprising word in the stanza — surprising not because unusual but because of its sound — it is "blank". Short 'a' followed by 'k' makes a sound with a crispness much at odds with the sound-patterning of the rest of the lines. Even the rhythm of the line accentuates it, the third of three long stresses, but the one on which the greatest stress seems to fall. But all this means nothing unless it has some interaction with the meaning of the words, and it does. The word that stands out most from among these twenty-seven monosyllables is the bleakest, emptiest word in the whole poem. It is as if the moon, symbol of love and fidelity, were an effaced coin, unavoidably present, but incapable of giving comfort, merely casting its light on the long road ahead.

If we ask the question 'How much of this was deliberately set up by Housman, and how much are we reading into it?' we might best answer in his own words, from the Leslie Stephen Lecture, and concerning the practice of poets in the art of versification: "and their success, when they succeed, is owing to instinctive tact and natural goodness of ear" (p.350). I merely want to leave you with another four lines, this time with two two-syllable words, which though not as well-written contain a pathos all of their own, one that seems inseparable from what we know of Housman's actual life, no matter how much we may want to read it otherwise, and which seems stronger for that:

> He would not stay for me; and who can wonder?
>   He would not stay for me to stand and gaze.
> I shook his hand and tore my heart in sunder
>   And went with half my life about my ways.

I have tried to resist biographical criticism, whilst attempting to give full notice of the issues inherent in the poems. I have come out realising that the more the poet was at pains to hide the biographical aspects of his work, the more I have been led to grub them up, to say how central they are to the poems. I hope I have only done this in order to explain difficulties inherent in the poems, and to bring to light issues which may be larger than the personal tragedy of one man writing poems as simple as Housman's are.

Carrollean Housman

Throughout his life, A.E. Housman was a regular writer of 'nonsense-verse', a steady output of poems often sent in letters to friends but decidedly not produced for publication, or with the thought of publication at all in mind. Only three of the longer of these pieces appeared during his lifetime, *Three Poems: The Parallelogram. The Amphisbaena. The Crocodile.*, a pamphlet he allowed to be privately printed by the Department of English, University College, London in 1935. At time of writing only a proportion of this material has yet seen print, and much more remains to be collected from scattered letters and papers in the forthcoming definitive edition of Housman's work being edited by Archie Burnett. So this is no more than a kind of interim report.

Despite the title of this chapter, I think there are decided differences between these verses and those of Carroll and Lear. As you might expect from the author of *A Shropshire Lad*, there is quite a lot of death in them; comical, but sometimes nasty. There is a kind of cruelty that reminds me more of what children sometimes write for themselves rather than what good Victorians wrote for their children. Significantly, like Dodgson and Barrie, Housman was childless, but unlike them he showed no need for the company of children and had no idealistic dreams about childhood. Not that he could not enjoy the company of children, as Grant Richards has testified, but there were limits. However, many of these pieces were written for the children of his sister Kate Symons, those that were not being usually for other members of his family. The following was sent to his stepmother when he heard that Laurence was to bring out a volume of 'Devotional Poems' in 1897. It is one of two that he wrote for the occasion:

'Hallelujah!' was the only observation
That escaped Lieutenant-Colonel Mary Jane,
When she tumbled off the platform in the station,
And was cut in little pieces by the train.
   Mary Jane, the train is through yer:
   Hallelujah, Hallelujah!
We will gather up the fragments that remain. (*P.&P.* p.239)

This irreverent send-up of the pious is a fairly typical example of Housman's wit, but it is not typical of his verse, by far the largest proportion of which is in the form of cautionary tales for children. 'The African Lion' is one of the best of these. The lion in question likes to eat bad boys, "But he rightly and strongly objects to the taste/Of good and uneatable boys". So in true Victorian fashion, goodness in children is rewarded, since the lion will find they taste nasty:

So lads of good habits, on coming across
   A lion, need feel no alarm,
For they know they are sure to escape with the loss
   Of a leg, or a head, or an arm.

                (*A.E.H.* p.240)

Most children come to a bad end, like William who tells a lie and turns purple (*P.&P.* p.250) or Eliza in 'Aunts and Nieces or, Time and Space' (*P.&P.* pp.251–52) who is knocked into the middle of next week by the "dangerous cockyoly bird":

In the middle of next week
There will be heard a piercing shriek,
And looking pale and weak and thin
Eliza will come flying in.

As I have said, this is certainly not the kind of nonsense Housman talked about in relation to 'pure' poetry. In fact I would say that nonsense is perhaps more appropriate a word for that context than for this. 'Nonsense verse' (Lear's and Carroll's included) tends to work by a specific set of operations in relation to sense itself. Either by inversion of the expected sense, or by taking sense literally ("the middle of next week") or by a pretence at sense and importance, as in Lewis Carroll's 'The Jabberwocky'. 'The Parallelogram or, Infant Optimism' is a delightful piece of literal-mindedness, describing the attributes of this particular quadrilateral:

> It does not scratch, it does not bite,
> It does not make a noise at night;
> It would attempt these acts in vain:
> And why? because it is a plane.

(*P.&P.* p.241)

Nothing could make more sense, only the act of telling it makes it ridiculous. 'The Amphisbaena or, the Limits of Human Knowledge' (*P.&P.* pp.243–44) is about a serpent with a head at each end, and the philosophical problem of knowing which is the front and which the back.

'The Crocodile or, Public Decency' (*P.&P.* pp.247–48) has a slightly satirical edge, making a similar kind of comment on Victorian hypocrisy as the cautionary tales. It concerns a good Victorian crocodile, scandalised by an infant running naked on the banks of the Nile:

> Oh infant! oh my country's shame!
> Suppose a European came!
> Picture his feelings, on his pure
> Personally conducted tour!
> The British Peer's averted look,
> The mantling blush of Messrs. Cook!
> Come, awful infant, come and be
> Dressed, if in nothing else, in me.

Naturally there follows a literal flood of crocodile tears.

The final category of Housmanian nonsense that I want to mention is the parody. One of these is the delightful skit on Greek Tragedy, (*P.&P.* pp.236–38) beginning with this speech by the Chorus:

> O suitably attired in leather boots
> Head of a traveller, wherefore seeking whom
> Whence by what way how purposed art thou come
> To this well-nightingaled vicinity?

144

At the other end of the scale is a parody of Blake, which incorporates the famous lines on the tyger:

O have you caught the tiger?
  And can you hold him tight?
And what immortal hand or eye
Could frame his fearful symmetry?
  And does he try to bite?

Again, somebody comes to a bad end, since "He has a less contented look/Than in the Natural History book,/And seems a trifle lean".

I suppose these are all nearer in tone to Kipling than anything else. The lions, elephants and tigers act out the Victorian fascination with the wilder fruits of Empire, and much of the humour comes from playing these off against cosy domestic attitudes. It is at any rate a fairly underestimated side of Housman's output, partly because the material has been hard to get hold of (until the recent publication of *Collected Poems and Selected Prose* which prints only a selection of what had already appeared in print) and partly because of the lack of this material in the first place. It seems that there is more on the way and it will soon become time to ask just how Housman compares with the likes of Lear, Carroll and others. He is certainly less of a writer for children, but I think he handles the form of light verse better, the telling rhyme, the sting in the tale of the punch-line.

Abbreviations

Works by Housman:

Unless otherwise cited, poems are quoted from *The Collected Poems of A.E. Housman* (Jonathan Cape, 1939, pbk 1967, still in print). Roman numerals refer to their position in the original individual volumes:

ASL – A Shropshire Lad
LP – Last Poems
MP – More Poems
AP – Additional Poems (see also Laurence Housman's *A.E.H.*).

P.&P.   *A.E. Housman: Collected Poems and Selected Prose*, ed. Christopher Ricks (Penguin, London, 1988)

SP   *A.E. Housman: Selected Prose*, ed. John Carter (Cambridge Univ. Press, 1961, 62)

CP   *The Classical Papers of A.E. Housman*, ed. J. Diggle & F.R.D. Goodyear (Cambridge Univ. Press, 1972)

Letters   *The Letters of A.E. Housman*, ed. Henry Maas (Rupert Hart-Davis, London, 1971).

Works on Housman, etc.:

A.E.H.   *A.E.H.: Some Poems, Some Letters and a Personal Memoir*, Laurence Housman (Jonathan Cape, London, 1937)

Brom.   *Alfred Edward Housman: Recollections*, Bromsgrove Memorial Supplement (*The Bromsgrovian*, 1936)

Chambers	*Man's Unconquerable Mind*, R.W. Chambers (Jonathan Cape, London, 1939)
C.O.	*Coming Out: Homosexual Politics in Britain, from the Nineteenth Century to the Present*, Jeffrey Weeks (Quartet Books, London, 1977)
De Amicitia	*A.E. Housman's 'De Amicitia'*, Laurence Housman, annotated by John Carter (*Encounter* Vol. XXIX No. 4, Oct. 1967)
Gow	*A.E. Housman: a Sketch*, A. S. F. Gow (Cambridge Univ. Press, 1936)
Graves	*A.E. Housman: The Scholar-Poet*, Richard Perceval Graves (Routledge & Kegan Paul, London, 1979; OUP pbk, 1981)
HSJ	*Housman Society Journal*
Marlow	*A.E. Housman: Scholar and Poet*, Norman Marlow (Routledge & Kegan Paul, 1958).
Naiditch	*A.E. Housman at University College: The Election of 1892*, P.G. Naiditch (E.J. Brill, Leiden, 1988)
Page	*A.E. Housman: a Critical Biography*, Norman Page (Macmillan, London, 1983, 85)
Richards	*A.E. Housman 1897–1936*, Grant Richards (Oxford Univ. Press, 1941)
Withers	*A Buried Life*, Percy Withers (Jonathan Cape, London, 1940)

Publisher's Acknowledgements

We are indebted to the following for permission to reproduce photographs: N.V.H. Symons and J.M.C. Pugh (1, 2, 5); Gerald Symons (6); the Master and Fellows of Trinity College, Cambridge (7, 10, 12, 13); Shropshire Records and Research Unit (8, 9); the National Portrait Gallery (11).